Hiking for Fun and Pain

David Curran

Hiking for Fun and Pain

ISBN 978-0-9859107-9-2

Oconee Spirit Press, Waverly, TN www.oconeespirit.com

Library of Congress Cataloging-in-Publication Data

Curran, David

Hiking for fun and pain/ David Curran

1. Hiking – New England. 2. Hiking - Great Smoky Mountains National Park (N.C. and Tenn.). 3. Hiking - Appalachian Trail. 4. Hiking - Rocky Mountain National Park (Colo.). 5. Hiking – Grand Teton National Park. 6. Hiking – Wyoming - Wind River Range.

10 9 8 7 6 5 4 3 2 1

Printed and bound in the United States. The text paper is SFI certified. The Sustainable Forestry Initiative® program promotes sustainable forest management.

Photographs by David Curran
Cover art copyright © gajus | 123RF
Cover design by Center Central Design

Dedication
To my beloved wife, Lola.

Note To Readers

The reader is urged to check on current situations on any hike undertaken, as manmade trails are altered over time. For example, in the first chapter, a hike to the fire tower at Greenbrier Pinnacle in the Smokies is described. Since then, the fire tower has been removed and the park no longer maintains that trail. Likewise the park has removed other fire towers such as the one at High Rocks and has blocked people from climbing the one at Shuckstack.

Periodically changes are made to the Appalachian Trail due to a variety of reasons. Additionally, the names of some individuals in this book have been changed to protect their privacy.

Table of Contents

The Discovery of New Vistas

Looking at the mother bear and her two cubs prowling around the shelter, I wondered about the wisdom of taking up hiking as a pastime. Robert, my frequent hiking partner, and I were trapped inside the shelter at Spence Field in the Great Smoky Mountains National Park, rather like two animals in a zoo watching those free on the outside. We had spent a grueling day hiking up Jenkins Ridge and stopped to spend the night at this shelter, even though our permit was for another shelter three miles further up the trail. The shelter was not full and we were prepared to pay the fine in the event a ranger came along and found us camping in the wilderness without proper authorization. What we hadn't counted on was the diverse amount of wildlife we would encounter that night.

Until recently, all the shelters in the Smokies were a three-sided log affair with a tin roof and two levels covered with chicken wire to support sleeping bags and their inhabitants. Each rack contained eight backpackers. The front of the shelter is open, but due to the problems of bears constantly entering the shelters in search of food to the great consternation of sleeping hikers, a chain link fence with a door covers the open end. The shelters are mainly on the Appalachian Trail to eliminate the need for tent sites for backpackers and to limit the environmental damage of excessive use. These shacks in the forest are definitely substandard housing by anyone's values, but they are luxury suites on the trail that afford protection from the weather for tired hikers and eliminate the need to set up a tent. But as in all wilderness experiences, they have their own unique challenges.

The mother bear with her two cubs made their appearance during our supper that night. As we were cooking and eating inside the protective confines of our shelter, this did not concern us greatly. However, momma bear was very persistent and kept returning throughout the night. At one point, while we were trying to sleep, the mother bear gripped with her teeth one of the backpack straps that was hanging through the fence. We watched with interest as the backpack bounced up and down as the bear made the futile effort to steal the pack and have a midnight snack. This bear had a very mean temper, and this ineffectual effort only seemed to make her madder. After the bear wandered off again, I settled down into a fitful sleep. Another six hikers were on the upper rack and Robert and I had decided to sleep on the lower rack. We slept on opposite sides of the rack with plenty of room between us in the event there were late-arriving backpackers. I was startled out of my sleep by some rustling noise nearby and low mummers from my follow hikers.

While the fence did keep out bears, it did not keep out smaller varmints, and I saw a skunk on the floor of the shelter looking for food among our gear. I watched its exploration with detached amusement and then with alarm when it jumped up to our bunk level. One of life's strange experiences is to go eyeball to eyeball with a skunk three feet away in the middle of the night. With a certain quiver in my voice, I said, "Robert, there is a skunk between us on this rack. What should we do?" Out of the darkness, Robert replied with a slow measured tone, "Don't....bother....it!" While the skunk continued its search, I reviewed our options. If the skunk decided to let go with its noxious spray, we couldn't stay in the shelter. Yet on the other hand, the ill-tempered mother bear and her two cubs could still be nearby. What to do, what to do? I finally decided if the skunk did use its arsenal, the only choice was to sleep on top of the shelter for the night. Happily, we were spared that fate when the skunk had satisfied its curiosity, jumped down and paraded arrogantly back into the forest.

However, Spence Field shelter had other trials for us. Where there is food, there will be a significant animal population, including mice. The shelters have become an ecological niche for wildlife that couldn't exist without the shelters at this stage of their evolution. I love all the little critters of the woods, but it is a bit unnerving at night to lie in a sleeping bag atop chicken wire and listen to the ping, ping, ping as mice run hither and yonder around your prostrate body. It certainly doesn't make for a restful night to realize you are sleeping in a sizable mouse nest. Precautions are also necessary to prevent the mice from getting into the backpacks to explore for food when it is kept in the shelter. After our dinner, most of us started hanging our backpacks from the ceiling or high on the chain link fence inside the shelter. A "rookie" at hiking asked why we were engaging in this strange ritual. He had his expensive new pack leaning against the fence. We explained the reason and offered to hang his pack up for him, but he cheerfully declined. The next morning there was a hole about the size of a silver dollar in the side of his backpack where a mouse had gnawed through to get to all the tempting food items. Another exciting night on the trail had passed.

My fascination with hiking lies deep in the traumas of my childhood. At a very early age, I developed rheumatic fever, which left me with a damaged heart. Because of its effects, I could not run and play with abandon, for, if I did, terrible pains in my ankles and knees came at night. It is unnatural for a young boy not to play sports. To learn discipline in the face of my condition required me to turn down invitations for games where there was no visible handicap and to stand aside from major social functions of childhood, a scarring experience for a young boy. When I did play hard, the torments would come at night and I developed a stoic attitude of not complaining about pain unless it became unbearable, which proved to be a helpful concept when I did take up hiking.

In my little rural town of Parkesburg, Pennsylvania, baseball was the game of choice for my friends, but even that was too much for me. My childhood companions were understanding and I was not harassed or bullied, but it is still a heavy burden to bear to not be a part of the normal activities. For exercise, I would walk, which was a distinctly strange pastime for a youth in the 1950s. Solitary long walks at such a young age leaves one with a philosophical leaning and some difficulty in being part of the group then and later. However, as a child I accepted this as my particular fate in life and determined to live around it without self-pity or bitterness.

The farms and forest around our small town were as tranquil as anyone could imagine and in my distant memory of childhood in the fifties that world exists as some Shangri-La of a long lost paradise. With friends or alone, it was a wonderful area to explore on foot. In the summer, I would have a brief breakfast, disappear until lunch, depart again and reappear at supper. My friends and I would often walk down back roads or forest trails for hours. Looking back on it all, I am amazed at the freedom we had, for our parents would not have had the slightest idea where we were. If we had ever gotten lost, to find us would have entailed a 360 degree search for several miles by the authorities.

Our home had a large yard with a creek in the back and fields beyond it. As so many things about my life were offset from the normal, it transpired that I acquired a duck for a pet instead of the usual stereotype of a young boy with his dog. My pet duck, Quacker, and I spent many a joyful hour together looking for crayfish in the creek and searching the fields for grasshoppers that Quacker would promptly devour. Quacker was loyal as any canine, and my mother would recount how each day the duck would leave the creek and come to our front gate to wait for me at the time I would return home from school so we could resume our discovery of life together. Someday, I will write the great American short story about a young boy coming of age with his pet duck and their special bond of trust and affection while exploring brooks and meadows.

When I was eleven, my step-father and mother decided to move to Florida, partly to help improve my health, for I was often sick. We eventually settled in Largo, near St. Petersburg and four miles from the Gulf of Mexico. Now Florida does not entice one to hike in the wilderness or even to stray very far from town. First there are the mosquitoes that come in swarms like emissaries of the dark side of nature. In the first town we lived in, Punta Gorda, I would come home from the movie theater at night and sense a shadow behind me, only to discover that it was a cloud of mosquitoes in the shape of my body trying to catch up with me for their evening repast. Furthermore, snakes inhabit any overgrown area, which is a definite discouragement to wandering in the woods or dales. As with all challenging situations, it can be fairly safe if proper measures are observed, but as a teenager I was not going to try without guidance. My walks were confined to the town, where people said they could set their clocks by the regularity of my strolls. The beaches were also wonderful places to walk to study marine life and teenage girls. As for sports, football is king in Florida and obviously one that I was not going to participate in but for which I became a fanatic. I was on the high school debate team and we placed third in the state, but there did not seem to be much recognition in that endeavor.

My step-father never believed in air conditioning and the Florida sun can fry your brain in the summer. Happily, he decided the best relief was to spend some time in the mountains of North Carolina. We never did any real hiking, but the vacations gave me a lifelong love of the mountains. After college, it was with joy that I could settle in the region when I got a job with the Tennessee Valley Authority in Knoxville, Tennessee. Through my teenage years, doctors continued to advise me to restrain my physical activities, and my choice of activities had resulted in a strange physique. Below my waist I had strong and powerful legs from all my walking, and above my waist I was thin and frail. However the Florida climate had allowed me to become healthy. After locating in Knoxville, I decided the responsible thing was to find a doctor for long-term care and have a physical examination. I was twenty-three years old and the doctor said, "There is nothing wrong with your heart and you can do what you want. We now know that in ninety-five percent of the cases, the effects of rheumatic fever are cured over time by the body itself." Dumbfounded I asked if there were any restrictions I should follow. He said, "Take it easy starting out and work slowly into activities. I wouldn't go out and climb Mt. Le Conte right away." That immediately became my goal.

Where to start? I felt like a person reborn, like one sentenced to prison for life and then found innocent and set free. That evening, I went down to the university track and jogged around it without fear of pain for the first time in my life. However, I soon discovered that never having played any sport, my athletic skills were nonexistent, so it would only lead to personal embarrassment to participate in competitive games such as trying out for a neighbor baseball team or chasing golf balls around man-made greens. The logical next step was to continue what I had been doing best and transform my walking to the next level and hike in the mountains. I was sharing an apartment with two college students, and my roommate Don was a doctoral candidate in geography, which is a marvelously useful kind of roommate to have for a venture into the mountains.

If you are an adult and going hiking for the first time, there is a certain level of anxiety. Will the trail be clear or will we get lost? Will I be strong enough and will my feet get sore? What if a bear attacks or a rattlesnake strikes out of the bushes? Due to my medical restrictions, I had never done anything strenuous before. However, I was reassured by the fact that two of us were going, as it generally should be in hiking, for the dangers of trailblazing alone became apparent as time passed. If a problem developed, Don would be there. For our hike, like any good geography student, he studied a topography map and decided that a place called Greenbrier Pinnacle in the Smokies would be a good choice. It would be a seven mile round trip hike, had a peak with a firetower on top and was well situated for outstanding views of the most rugged section of the park.

We started one fine spring day, and I was delighted to be walking in the woods enjoying the forest and its serenity with only sound of birds. It was a librating moment for me to be doing something that had only been a fantasy before. Here I was in the wilderness, striding along as if my childhood of pain and restrictions had never existed. However, a certain level of reality set in as we continued up hill on many switchbacks. When one grows up in Florida, walking up a grade for any distance is a totally alien experience. I had walked a lot, but as this trail had a 2000 foot elevation gain I learned for the first time the implications of that in any hiking trail. A three-and-a-half mile uphill hike is more demanding than a six mile walk on a flat surface. After a while, I was prodding along with my tongue hanging out and for the first time came thoughts that would occupy my mind on many subsequent hikes where the exertion factor overpowers the pleasure principal. "What I am doing here? Why am I exhausted doing something I thought was for fun? I am never going to do this again!" In due time, we arrived at the top and were greatly rewarded with the fine views from the tower. The many mountains around me in their magnificence transported me beyond my fatigue and lifted me to a new dimension of life. It is strange that one can obtain similar mountain views by driving the scenic parkways in the area, but a view that one has struggled and sweated for has a transcendental compensation that is beyond one that requires no effort.

Encouraged by our first successful hike, we quickly planned another. Don, the intrepid map interpreter, suggested English Mountain, a massif outside the park, but parallel to the main range of the Smokies and also with a fire tower on top. It, too, spoke of wonderful views. TVA had detailed topo maps on all the area, and I purchased one for our chosen destination. This map was several years old, but we found a trail on the map that boldly led to the top. However it did begin off a rugged gravel road some distance from the main highway. We were going in Don's

Volkswagen and he had supreme confidence in its ability to handle the rutted and rocky road that we encountered.

After driving down the wretched road that was almost a cattle path, we found the place shown on the map for the trail and started up the overgrown manway. Soon there was no trail at all, and we were faced with a choice of going back or bludgeoning ahead in a new adventure. At that time, I did not know how difficult hiking off trail can be in the Smokies, for a six mile hike off trail in the park can wear out the best conditioned young hiker in short order. However, English Mountain is not in the park and had been logged extensively over the years and lacked the true wilderness quality of much of the park. Because it had been logged, it lacked the thick undergrowth of vegetation that is so common in virgin forest. Nevertheless, to get to the top of the main ridge line, we had to climb up the rugged face of the mountain by pulling ourselves up rocks and boulders and carefully considering each foothold so as not to have a quick unplanned trip down the mountain. We reached the ridge top and proceeded to walk through the forest. I was growing in uncertainty of the whole endeavor. Don's version of the events was that we were "following the topo lines," and my storyline was that we were lost. But while English Mountain is large it lacks a complicated topography so at worst all we had to do was head downhill in any direction to come to a road. Being novices at hiking, we only had Don's single canteen of water, and the food we had was pretzels. When one hikes in the heat with limited water, salty pretzels are not a good choice of food and soon I had drunk all of the water in Don's canteen, an occurrence that lead to some irrational annoyance on his part (at least from my point of view) and an offense I would hear about for some time.

Hiking in our thirsty state, we had not even reached the fire tower yet, when seemingly miraculously we encountered a gravel road on the ridge top which was a wondrous sight for two wandering in the wilderness. After enjoying the breathtaking views from the fire tower of the main line of the Smokies laid out in front of us, it was time to start back. Don was all in favor of going cross country again, but I wanted to cling to the dirt road like a life vest. He pointed out that while the dirt road would take us to the road where our car was, we would still be three miles from the car when we hit the main rutty road. With concern about hiking in the dark, I prevailed over the implied insult to his navigational skills as a geographer, and down the road we went with a one sided discussion of our thirst and my sin of draining the last drop of water from the canteen. As we got to the base of the mountain we happily found a spring, and the water from it was the sweetest tasting liquid on the face of the earth.

When we came to the main road, which was a pitiful excuse for a path for cars, we started up it to our vehicle. As we meandered up this road we noted that many bridges were washed out, but my interest in such things was flagging as weariness was taking precedent over ordinary thoughts. Then, in a dust cloud appeared an old pickup truck, and from it emerged two bearded mountaineers. They could have been cast later in the movie *Deliverance*, but they seemed congenial enough. They inquired about the road ahead and we informed them it was impassable. They asked how we had gotten here and we explained, pointing out the cliff side we had climbed that morning.

They surveyed the side and one said, "I sure killed a lot of rattle-snakes up there," which had a distinctly unsettling feeling for me as I recalled our reaching up from one rock to another as we went up the side, putting our hands above us where we could not see what lurked there. One remarked to the other, "Well why don't we give these boys a ride back to their car."

As I got in the truck, a shotgun was propped up in the center of the seat, but I thought if they wanted my money, they could have it as long as they dropped us off at the car. But, as with so many mountain people, when treated with respect they were good hearted souls who helped us out in our time of need.

However, the two hikes were full of lessons to apply in the future and reinforced in me the desire to go once again into the woods and see the wonders of the forest, for the tranquilly of the soul it brings and the inspiration of the views from the top after the summit has been obtained. At the same time I realized that this was an undertaking not to be taken too lightly, and good planning and physical conditioning are critical.

The Challenge of Mt. Le Conte

The Great Smoky Mountains National Park is the most popular park in the United States, attracting over ten million visitors a year. Visitation could be higher, but some of the multitudes never make it beyond the shops and tourist attractions of Gatlinburg, Pigeon Forge and Cherokee. The Park has over 500,000 acres, with its most dominant feature being the majestic ridgeline of peaks that march in a continuous procession for thirty-six miles, all above 5000 feet. Unlike most western parks, none of the land was federally owned until a movement occurred early in the twentieth century to have a national park in the east.

The Great Smoky Mountains were the obvious choice for such a park and Congress approved its establishment in 1926, but, in its wisdom, neglected to approve any funds for land acquisition. The land was owned by small farmers and the lumber companies and to purchase the property would require more than ten million dollars, a huge sum for the 1920s and the following depression years of the 1930s. The people of Tennessee and North Carolina, through personal donations and state funds, managed to raise five million for this endeavor they so fervently desired. However the effort appeared to falter halfway to the goal. Incredibly, John D Rockefeller II came forward and matched the amount with a donation of five million dollars of his own wealth. With the money available, the slow and sad process of acquiring the land from the small farmers and moving them off the land commenced, as well as the urgent task of purchasing the holdings of the lumber companies before the remaining virgin forest was logged over and decimated.

In 1940 President Roosevelt dedicated the park at Newfound Gap. As I hike in the park, I have frequently reflected on the people of North Carolina and Tennessee, poor as they were then, who struggled to raise the money for this magnificent wilderness and the great generosity of Mr. Rockefeller to make such an endowment.

Of all the mountains in the Great Smoky Mountains National Park, one peak surpasses the others in its solitary glory: Mt. Le Conte at 6,593 feet is the third highest in the park, but it stands apart from the crest of the other summits in its own splendid isolation as a complete mountain unto itself. With its distinctive apex of three humps, it rises nearly a mile in front of the tourist utopia of Gatlinburg. Mt. Le Conte was the early focus in the attempt to establish the national park, commencing with the building of a primitive lodge in the 1920s near the top to encourage people to explore and experience the beauty of the wilderness. The lodge remains and is accessible only by foot or horseback, yet it is presently more like a small village with the accumulation of several additional cabins and support buildings. Mt. Le Conte is draped with five trails to the top that are frequently crowded—but a rugged wilderness off the trail.

My first hike to the top of Mt. Le Conte was about six months after I received the liberating news that I could physically do what I wanted with a caution to apply moderation. I had earlier been on three other hikes and felt I was ready for the looming hulk of Mt. Le Conte, so an outing was arranged with a co-op student sharing our apartment and his friend. The initial part of the Alum Cave Bluff trail is a pleasant stroll along a mountain stream, but it starts a steady climb after the first mile. It wasn't long into the trek that I quickly learned another important lesson about hiking: the significance of carefully choosing hiking partners. My two cohorts were tall athletic types with a competitive nature. Neither one wanted to be viewed as a wimp by the other, a contest of which I was not a part. After Alum Cave, they set a pace that would do credit to any of the Ridgerunners who explore this area. Their powerful long strides up the steep trail were more than I could equal, causing me to drop further and further behind until I was hiking by myself in this wilderness. At this immature stage of my wilderness proficiency, I did not welcome solitude. Occasionally, my companions would take a break and I would come puffing up the trail to their resting spot. When I reached them, my exhausted and hangdog look had no effect and they would jump up and say, "OK, let's go on." I wanted a rest for myself, but pride and embarrassment silenced my lips. This demeaning and demoralizing procedure repeated itself several times until, mercifully, the top was reached. Alas, another lesson about hiking was revealed with the discovery that the summit was totally in clouds, so no inspiring vistas were there to reward our laborious efforts. Not all hikes consent to the visions of Elysian Fields we possess before we set foot on the path.

On the way back, I could keep up with them on the semi-controlled race down the slopes. Even this was still not challenging enough for one and he suggested we go cross country following a mountain brook downhill. Happily the other partner didn't want to do this and some time later we met our other hiker at the bottom. Evidently, this side trip satisfied his longing to test his manhood against the terrain for he had a look of total fatigue and a ragged appearance to his clothes. After that experience, I tried to select hiking partners in my same general state of fitness and who liked to trudge at my slow uphill plod.

The Alum Cave Bluff trail we had used is 5 ½ miles and very steep after the first mile for a total elevation gain of 2560 feet. After sauntering nearly half of the trails in the park, I still consider the Alum Cave trail as the best of all pathways in the Smokies because of the variety of attractive features it possesses in its relatively short distance. Its own merits contribute to its major drawback, for the trail can be very crowded during peak hiking times, thus robbing it of the solitude that so many seek in the wilderness. Nevertheless, the first mile is a pleasant and relaxing stroll along a mountain stream with the soothing sounds of water bubbling downhill providing a calming hum so tranquil that tapes of it are sold in yuppie stores.

Even on such an innocuous stretch of path, a dark fate can await if proper precautions are not followed. One general rule is don't hike alone, and one absolute rule is, when hiking in the winter be prepared with proper attire for wintry weather. Near sunset one winter day, a man decided to hike up this trail, but was lightly dressed. Hypothermia is a condition where the body starts to lose heat faster than it can be replaced which quickly and insidiously affects the mental state by creating confusion and apathy. Apparently, this individual met the demons of the penetrating cold in this short two mile hike; at least that is what the park rangers believe happened when his body was found the next day. Winter hiking can be most enjoyable for the new vistas and increased solitude, but its unique challenge extracts a serious toll for the unwary that might not arise if one hikes ill-equipped in the summer.

After the first section of the Alum Cave Bluff trail, one comes to Arch Rock, which is a huge boulder that has split asunder, looming like a ruined medieval castle wall breached by Norse invaders. One crosses a wooden footbridge in front and once inside, climbs up stairs with a cable for hand support, so this cool dark passage creates no problem provided you remember another safety rule that wet rocks are slippery rocks. The trail gradually climbs to a pleasant overlook of the surrounding valley and a third of a mile beyond is Alum Cave Bluffs. The Bluffs are not a true cave but an impressive rocky overhang one hundred feet high with alum at the base formed over geologic time. This is about the halfway point to the top of Mt. Le Conte and a popular destination for day hikers.

Even though the round trip hike to Alum Cave is less than five miles, it can create unforeseen contingencies for those unwise enough to lead in-laws on it. Several years ago and early in our married life, I took my wife's brother, sister and aunt up this trail while my wife remained at home to entertain the less ambitious of her relatives visiting us. All three of my guests were adults in reasonably good physical condition; however being from mid-Missouri, which is fairly flat, they were not accustomed to uphill hiking. When we reached the overlook after some two miles and with the Bluffs in sight, my sister-in-law staged a mutiny and refused to go on, whereupon the other two staged a counter mutiny to plunge forward to our destination. What to do? What to do? After considerable negotiation, I extracted a promise from my sister-in-law to stay at the overlook until we returned from the Bluffs. As there were many hikers that day, I did not think that would create a problem. With some uncertainty as to the proper course of action, I led the rest of our party out to a most agreeable visit to the Bluffs. Lo, on the return, no sister-in-law at the overlook. After scouting around the area, including looking down the side of the mountain, I could only conclude she started back without us. On the hurried march down the trail, I reflected on now to explain to my wife that her brother and aunt had a great time but we lost her sister, and I was sure the park rangers would mount a determined search for her. When we got to the parking lot, there was sister waiting for us. She blithely explained that another party came by and she decided to follow them down. Harsh words on my part were stayed by the knowledge of the wifely consequences of such an imprudent action.

After the Bluffs, the continuous steep part of the trail begins until relief and exuberance is found at the top of Mt. Le Conte. This section of the trail sometimes is ravaged by storms and floods that require the trail to be relocated around problem areas. A trail can seem permanent, but it requires regular maintenance or natural forces would obviate it all. It makes one wonder how long the constructions of man would last in the face of Nature's forces if man ceased to exist. Additionally, there are many mysteries in the mountains, and this segment has its share. At one point the narrow trail clings to a rock wall on one side, three feet of uneven rocks, and then a precipitous slope with a magnificent view. On one winter day, two experienced backpackers came this way, hiking out of sight of each other as frequently occurs when each seeks his quietude in the chill. Eventually the first backpacker noticed the absence of the other and in the ensuing search his partner was found dead at the bottom of this cliff. One can only speculate on such a solitary death. A prevailing theory is that the backpacker paused to enjoy the view at this point, took off his pack to rest, and when he swung his pack back on he lost his balance and went over the side of the cliff. Among such beauty exists sobering reminders of our own mortality.

The top of Mt. Le Conte consists of three peaks that are very distinctive when approaching the mountains through Pigeon Forge. The Mt. Le Conte Lodge remains a prime destination at the summit. The first time my wife and I arrived there to stay overnight, we staggered into the dining hall to register. One of the employees brought out a large pail of water and said it was for us. We laughed, thinking he was assuming we were very thirsty, but he declared, without a smile, that the bucket of water was for our cabin. We soon discovered it was indeed a primitive lodge without running water, bathroom or electricity in the cabins. Everyone ate family style in the dining hall, with delicious food prepared by the capable staff. The community outhouse was down the path from the cabin, but we decided not to make any midnight trek to it after a bear walked by our cabin at dusk when we were settling down. Social activities are limited at the lodge, with the major event being the short hike up to Cliff Top to view the sunset. Of course, one is so tired that not much else is expected. For the truly ambitious there is the half mile predawn hike to Myrtle Point to watch the sunrise, an event not nearly as well attended as the sunset.

Getting supplies to Le Conte Lodge is always a challenge for the managers considering there are no roads to it. Helicopters have been used, as well as the more traditional way of bringing the supplies by horseback or backpacking them in by means of the hardy staff. Recently a more innovative approach has been to use llamas for transport. Llamas have several advantages, the biggest one being that they have padded feet that do not tear up the trails like horse hooves will. Still, it leaves one with a strange feeling to be hiking to Grotto Falls on the Trillum Gap Trail and be confronted with a handler bringing four llamas down the trail. This startling event makes you want to check the map again to make sure you are not on some South American trail.

There is also a shelter at Mt Le Conte a short distance from the lodge. Robert and I decided to use it on a weekend hike, utilizing some of the mountain trails we did not normally traverse. The recurring theme of the importance of weather conditions once again came into focus. It was the last weekend in March and in Tennessee winter is usually past, but the top of Mt. Le Conte is more similar to Canada than the South, a fact easily overlooked by us dwellers of the lower elevation. We knew a weather front was approaching, but as we both had scheduled this weekend for the hike and as we had the appropriate approvals from our wives, we pressed ahead. We took two cars in order to cover more trails and to start at the higher elevation. I parked my car at the end of Trillium Gap Trail, which is at elevation of 3100 feet, piled my gear in Robert's car and then we drove to Newfound Gap, which is at 5040 feet. As the Mt. Le Conte shelter is at 6400 feet, we had only a 1400-foot gain as opposed to the 3300-foot gain if we started at Trillium Gap. It is not necessary that all hiking be pain and while we often opt for the lesser challenge, nevertheless we would hike fourteen miles in two days with a pack of winter gear.

The hike along the Appalachian Trial and the Boulevard Trial was uneventful except for the steadily worsening weather and the apprehension that we would find ice on the trail as we approached Le Conte. Foremost in my mind was an experience of a friend who hiked this section in winter and found the trail covered with ice near the end. He got down on all fours to crawl across the ice, but as the trail had a downward pitch at that point, he had the unsettling dilemma of constantly sliding toward the oblivion below. If we couldn't get through at the very end we faced the prospect of hiking eight miles back to our car in the dark. Happily the trail was passable and happier still there was room for us at the shelter.

The night came as a wintry one and so did four inches of snow despite being almost April. As a shelter is open on one side, the inside temperature is the same as the outside, and in the course of this cold night I discovered that my sleeping bag was not as efficient as I had hoped. One does not sleep well while shivering, even when wearing all the clothes and the coat you brought with you and you are withdrawn into the deepest recesses of the sack. In the morning, we discovered that the water had frozen in our canteens, and in any event we were not in a mood to try to prepare breakfast in such frigid conditions. After leaving the shelter in some haste, we were further stressed by our inability to find the terminus of the Trillium Trail. While the Mt. Le Conte Lodge is closed to the public in the winter, a staff stays there year round to maintain the facility as well as to protect it from vandalism by very cold and unscrupulous hikers who break into the cabins in the winter because their sleeping bags are inadequate. We knocked on the door and politely enquired about the directions to Trillium, and I was unable to resist asking if we could also have some hot tea even if they were not open for business. We were kindly invited into the toasty lodge and as we savored the warming beverages in our bodies, our other senses were assaulted by the aroma of bacon and eggs being prepared by lodge staff. I decided it would be impolite to attempt to further impose on their generosity by imitating Oliver Twist in an abject request for food.

The forest with a fresh wet blanket of snow is a very quiet place when there is no wind, and there is a serene beauty that one can only find in the natural world. After getting pointed in the right direction, we lumbered down the Trillium Trail. The exercise removed our coldness and we walked in the silence befitting our surroundings, in peace with the world. At the midway point of our trek, the mood changed as we left the snow-covered forest for wet and bleak woods that had a depressing quality. Finally we reached my car, which was unaffected by what had occurred above us. On the other hand, Robert's car at Newfound Gap wasn't going anywhere for a while, as the road to the Gap was closed by snow and ice. We traveled home to Knoxville and came back the next day after work to retrieve his car —for the snow melts fast that time of year— and it was no worse for having spent an extra night at Newfound Gap.

Part of the joy of hiking is that when one is away from the more crowded trails, a sense of camaraderie sets in among hikers and back-packers, and we frequently chatted with people along the way. On one occasion, Robert and I were on the Boulevard trail when we stopped to converse with an older man and three others. We discovered he was Dr. Sharpe, a well-known retired botanist from the University of Tennessee. He related that he had hiked to the top of Mt. Le Conte over 120 times and then he introduced his party, "We are four generations making this hike. This is my daughter, my grandson and my great grandson." We could only walk away in awe, and wonder if we would be able to do that kind of hiking if we reached his age.

The ambiance of a trail can be ever-changing as the same path can yield radically different experiences with each season revealing unique characteristics or even with different weather conditions creating distinc-tive moods. A favorite destination in the park is Rainbow Falls, which is the highest waterfall in the park in terms of a straight drop for some hundred feet, as distinct from cascades that may be higher, but the water battles with rocks all the way down. Rainbow Falls has presented a different appearance every time I have been there. If considerable rain has occurred over several weeks, likely there will be an impressive volume of water surging over the top to the churning maelstrom below, with a hazy mist shrouding the approach. On the other hand, after a dry period, Rainbow Falls can be just pathetic little individual streams of water dripping down like so many leaky faucets. In summer, the Falls are clothed in the greenery it nurtures, but in winter other moods can come. In one particularly cold February, we saw in the newspaper that the Falls had frozen, so Robert and I decided to witness this for ourselves. One of the major challenges of winter hiking is the drive to the trailhead. The beginning of the trail is only three miles from the center of Gatlinburg, but the road is uphill and I was driving my big Buick Century which does not handle well in icy conditions. We were forced to park the car halfway up the snow-covered road and began walking, but happily a kindly soul gave us a ride after we had ventured only a short distance. The trail to Rainbow Falls is never a good one, being over-used by hikers and previously by horse trains taking supplies to Mt. Le Conte. However, when we did arrive at the Falls we were greeted with the sight of a soaring blue column of ice instead of the torrent of water we were accustomed to seeing. It was not as aesthetically pleasing as I would have liked, with the frozen pillar being somewhat lopsided, but it was imposing nevertheless. It is for such sights that one returns to the same place in different seasons to realize Nature's ever-changing moods.

Early in our hiking career, in order to condition ourselves for our first overnight trip, Robert and I hiked up the Rainbow Falls Trail and down the Bullhead trail. Those two connecting trails constituted a total of thirteen miles and nearly a 4000-foot elevation gain, a trip guaranteed to build you up or cure you of any further desire to hike when you are a novice in this sport. I was disgruntled on the journey upward as I had been anticipating the many views that these trails offer, but we were fated to hike in haze and fog the whole day. However, it is important to appreciate what is offered, and frequently what seems to be a disappointing day has its unexpected delights. After our obligatory visit to Le Conte Lodge, we started down the Bullhead Trail. Now I am not a person who raptures over flowers, but that day I was enthralled by the abundance of wild blooms that were profuse on this trail. It was like walking in a garden where the keeper had scattered randomly his best specimens at odd and unexpected turns, waiting for the traveler to delight in their discovery.

In all hiking circles there is a strong injunction not to hike alone, but it is discarded by even the seasoned hiker under certain circumstances or abandoned for the sheer challenge. One fine August day I hiked alone on Alum Cave Trail to the top of Mt. Le Conte and back for the novelty of experiencing this trail for the first time in solitude. However, I did not really hike alone as there were at least 200 people on the trail that day, so safety was not an issue unless I left the trail. To enjoy any hike, one must take what is encountered on that day and discard expectations, for if you cling only to your anticipations you will not benefit from what is offered. Normally I hike for solitude of the wilderness to be away from the crowds of everyday life. On this trip up the mountain, there was a continuous stream of people hiking up to the peak or coming down from a night at the lodge. Because of the time of year, I knew there would be many people, but did not expect to have the feeling of being in a march of army ants in the jungle seeking new horizons. The normally serene Alum Cave Bluffs had several groups clustered around the base, as if several tribes of nature-worshippers had arranged this spot for a camp gathering.

There is a balance in life, and while one side of me seeks isolation from human activity another side relishes the discourse with those of shared interest and to once again tell my favorite anecdotes to those who have not had the honor of hearing them and to marvel at their sagas. This day was to be a day of sharing and not of separation. Prior to Arch Rock, I crossed a log bridge where I saw a person standing motionless beside the stream. In a low voice, the man said he had just crossed a minute ago, looked up and saw a bobcat sitting on the rock. It was graceful when it scrambled back into the woods. That was indeed a rare encounter, for I have never seen any cat or cougar in the wilds. The man was Stan from Orlando and I chatted with him occasionally the entire day as our pace quickened or slackened and we led or followed on the trail. I related to him my story of Dr. Sharpe with his more than one hundred times up Le Conte, and then Stan asked me if I had heard of Ed Wright, who has made over 1200 hikes to the top of Le Conte and who has his own web page about this obsession. One's stories can always be trumped.

My major discovery on this hike is how willing people are to talk to a solo hiker. Being alone on the trail paradoxically merely increases the opportunity, the temptation and the necessity to converse with others. The true solitaire on the trail merely grunts at others, but that is not my nature. Social contacts on the trail are far different than in the "real" world. Few would consider talking to a total stranger walking down an urban street, but in the forest there are few such inhibitions. For one thing, we all share in common the pursuit of walking in a more demanding venture than we normally undertake, which leads to a casual bonding of kindred souls. People you meet rarely have any hidden agendas, so no one is becoming friendly for a self-seeking goal, such as inviting you to a meeting in order to explain some great business opportunity. Our contacts will be ephemeral, for a minute to a few hours at most, but for a brief scan of time we are one in a common pursuit. Thus the trip to the top was filled with many conversations as well as sitting in the rocking chair at the primitive lodge and discoursing with fellow travelers as if it were the eighteenth century sans radio, television or computer.

Due to the lateness of the hour of my return from the top of Mt Conte, I found myself hiking for long periods without meeting others on the trail. Fatigue always changes one's perspective on any undertaking, and as I paused for a snack the forest that was so warm and welcoming as I traveled upward became a dark and foreboding presence on this lonely descent with dusk approaching. My mind started imagining bears and mountain lions secretly watching me and preparing to pounce upon such easy prey as a straggler unprotected by the herd. I resolved at that time that while I would solo hike again I would not camp alone, if for no other reason than to keep my mind from journeying down its own dark passages of fears. As I approached Alum Cave Bluffs again I felt an ease coming over me, knowing that soon it would be an easy saunter to the parking lot, when I encountered a young woman hiking up to the Le Conte Lodge at this late hour to join her friends who worked there. Two strangers on the trail can have immediate rapport that would be rare in normal urban life. In the course of our rambling conservation, I learned that she was a recent college graduate and now certified to teach but was taking several months to travel and work at odd jobs before committing to the routines of the work world and married life. I told my story about having heart trouble as a youth to which she related that she had a degenerative heart condition that would shortly prevent her from this type of strenuous activity. Therefore she was hiking as much as she could before health eliminated this option in her life. Her cheery countenance in the face of grim reality left me with an inner glow for those who refuse to allow health limitations to impose despair. The richness of the forest is complemented by the fullness of spirit of those one meets on the trail.

In the course of all my hiking, no summit has more memories and meaning to me than this solitary peak of Mt. Le Conte. It was the first major mountain I climbed and if I can plan it, will be the last before the infirmities of years steal from me the option to select my destiny in life. Mt. Le Conte has become a special part in the fiber of my being; it is a personality and a presence like a lifelong friend.

Wildlife on the Trail and in the House

Part of the charm of the wilderness is an encounter with animals on the trail and, to a lesser joy, when they join you at your campsite. With animals, you are a transient guest in their abode and need to observe their standards, providing you aren't expected to provide food or be food for their repast. For humans meeting other species in their domain, the encounters are at a rare level of equality and perhaps inferiority, for you come unarmed in a national park and the animals understand this at some primeval level. The claws that scratch, the hoofs that gash and the teeth that bite are far more formidable than a puny hiking stick.

Many of the meetings with other creatures are so unexpected and surreal that they lend a dimension to life not likely to be experienced otherwise. The North Carolina part of the park has far fewer hikers than the Tennessee side, and consequently you hike in highly-valued solitude. Robert and I were on a five-day loop hike that started at Clingmans Dome, the highest point in the park and descended the whole length of Hazel Creek to where it emptied into Fontana Lake, and then came back uphill again to the Dome. On our third day out, we were very slowly ascending in a driving rain headed to the High Rocks fire tower for its view and then on to a campsite for the night. It was late in the day when we reached the fire tower and there was no view to be seen in the storm. Rather than go on to our reserved campsite in our soggy and exhausted state, we determined to stay at the abandoned cabin at the base of the fire tower and once again to risk the remote possibility of a fine if our wilderness meeting was with a ranger. The one-room cabin for fire rangers at High Rocks was a modest affair even when it was used, but we found it in a state of disrepair with no furniture and the entrance open to all the little creatures of the woods. After our supper, we wearily decided to go to sleep, even though there was considerable daylight remaining.

One's evening entertainment options in the forest are limited despite all the movies that show people singing around a blazing campfire. We were usually too tired to lift our voice in song or for that matter to gather all the down wood required for an unnecessary roaring conflagration.

To settle in for the night, we placed the discarded door back in its proper place to keep out unwanted visitors and climbed into our sleeping bags on the floor. However, after about an hour's sleep I awoke with an eerie feeling; something didn't seem right. I became aware of a gentle breeze across my face on an irregular basis and, as there was still light coming in the cabin, I noticed shadows flashing by the windows. What could be causing this strange phenomenon? Whatever it was, it was INSIDE the cabin WITH US! Then the terrible truth occurred to me; there were bats flying around the confined cabin and they wanted out for their nocturnal safari. With a somewhat shrill and unsteady voice, I said, "Robert, there are bats in here. I'm going to take down the door so they can fly out." Down went the door, out went the bats and up went the door again. The next morning I saw through the window our winged furry friends flying around, wanting to get inside for the day. I refused to open the door. They found somewhere else to settle for the day, and when we left we took down the door so they could reclaim their home. As Robert and I walked away from the cabin we joked that most people let the cat out before going to bed, but it had been our duty to let the bats out for the night.

Nevertheless, all animals must be treated with great respect and caution in the woods. Deer can provide a wallop with their hoofs and we all know what an angry skunk can do. There are even wild boars in the Great Smoky Mountains National Park. Boars are not native to the area, but were brought to the area from Europe early in the twentieth century in an attempt to set up an exotic hunting preserve. When the venture failed, it was decided to kill off the boars within the fenced preserve, but the boars had other ideas. Foolish men and brave dogs went in to exterminate them and when the argument was over, the dogs were dead, the men were in the trees and the boars had a mass breakout for the freedom of the deep forest. In those days, domestic pigs would roam freely and after the pigs and the boars became acquainted, their offspring established themselves in the area and eventually moved into park lands.

As hunting is not allowed in the national park, the boars correctly determined they had little to fear from harmless hikers. On one occasion while hiking on the Appalachian Trail I was walking wearily along in front, staring only at the ground immediately in front of me, when Robert said slowly and quietly, "Ah Dave, you might want to look up." There about twenty feet in front of me was a wild boar in the middle of the trail happily grazing on roots. I froze for a moment, but as the boar seemed undisturbed by our presence, I eased closer to snap some pictures, taking the precaution of unbuckling my backpack so I could drop it and climb a tree in case the boar took exception to our activities. After taking all the pictures I wanted and growing somewhat bored, we were faced with the problem that the boar was still in the trail and there was no good away around him. To encourage him to look for roots elsewhere, we slowly walked towards him and he slowly moved away, still grubbing for food all the time. This went on several times until he tired of the game, grunted and ran off into the woods, and we felt triumph when we were safely beyond his sanctuary.

Unknown to us, the boars would also hang around the shelters at night. I discovered this one dark evening when, after finishing supper, I went outside for the ceremonial throwing away of the apple core. Normally, I pack out all trash, but I figured an apple core would be a welcome addition to some critter's diet. I walked a short distance into the eerie forest and gave it a good heave. Immediately my hair stood on end when I heard a loud grunt in the direction of the thrown apple. This was instantly followed by the thunder of human feet and swine hoofs crashing though the underbrush. I am not sure whether the boar charged or retreated, but I made it back to the shelter in record time.

The boars, while not native to the area, might not pose a big problem except for their feeding habits. They feast by plowing up the ground to eat all edible plants, including several on the endangered list. The Park Service, in order to control the boars, eventually sent out rangers to hunt them, but these crafty swine are almost impossible to eradicate—the park can only contain them to a certain level. After this policy was instituted seeing boars became a rare event, but their presence was still apparent in the existence of ground that looks like someone used a rototiller on it. This policy is not well publicized, but we found out about it when we unexpectedly encountered a ranger carrying a rifle. He had been out a week, looked exhausted, and hadn't gotten any boars in his sights.

In discussing the boar problem with George Minnigh of the Park Service, he stated the hog removal program was started in the 1980s and they recently have killed the ten-thousandth pig. In 1986 they killed 1146, and as the program thins out the hogs the numbers have dropped, for in 2001 they killed only 241. Currently, the termination of boars averages 250-300 a year. Dr. Dick Lancia had made a study and determined that if the Park Service manages to kill half of them in a year, the population will be at a stable level. George thinks there are about 660 hogs in the park, based on the number they have been killing. Some ethically-challenged people have even introduced hogs illegally to the park because they like to keep the boar population up for illicit hunting purposes. There are six rangers battling gamely fulltime on hog control and other problem animals in the park. I asked a park ranger if other animals are disturbed by gun shots in the park as the rangers go after the boars. I could image other wildlife scattering for miles around after hearing a fire arm go off. He chuckled and said, "For the bears, it is like ringing a dinner bell as they come charging to feed on the fresh pork before the ranger can get to the dead boar." Bears are very smart in their own way.

There are many animals that have very successfully adapted to man's presence and will be found in the lowlands of the suburbs as well as the highlands of nature preserves. The skunk, with its formal defenses against man and dog, has had little problem establishing its dominance and proceeds about its life with a cavalier disregard for mankind that is degrading to the allegedly superior human species. After relating my experience of the skunk at Spence Field shelter to George Minnigh, he trumped my skunk story with one of his own that further demonstrated the skunk's indifference to people. George was in a shelter with the door open and working alone while two coworkers were elsewhere. While sitting by the fire place, he looked down to see a skunk sniffing at his shoe. He didn't move but then the skunk climbed deliberately up his pants leg, walked across his lap as if he were a convenient tree stump and proceeded to investigate the level next to them. The skunk left without incident. I complemented him on his self-discipline and he said there wasn't much choice considering the dire consequence if he reacted. George observed that skunks in the park are very docile and aren't a problem unless you make an issue of it — certainly an encounter any hiker would lose.

One has the feeling that some animals will be here in forest, field and urban asphalt long after man has departed the scene. The opossum is another raider of unattended food in the park and one that appears stupid. However, the opossum is nearly indestructible in man's alteration of the environment. I rarely see opossums in the wilds, but I encounter them regularly in my suburban home. My neighbor has a chain link fence around his backyard and for several years kept two cute little dogs there. As I do not have a canine, they served the very useful purpose of additionally watching my property for any intruders. I also have a fenced-in backyard and many a night I would hear our little doggy friends raising such a howl that I would assume the four horsemen of the Apocalypse had arrived. Invariably upon checking it was an opossum walking along the top of the fence going about its nightly rounds. On one occasion, the racket was longer than usual, and I arose at four in the morning to check on the matter. A very young opossum had gotten into the yard and was trapped in a corner of the fence facing the two ferociously barking dogs with no means to escape. It faced them down by snarling threateningly at one and then the other and the dogs were not about to tackle even such a small but aroused animal prepared to fight to the death. No playing dead this opossum. I was in a dilemma about what to do because to reach down into that melee of three sets of teeth and claws to lift out the opossum would be disastrous to my arm. Eventually I just went back to bed until the owner called in his pets and the young opossum left with a lesson about checking yards first for dogs.

Having opossums around adds a nice touch of the natural world to remind me of ever present longing to escape into the woods. However there are limits to how close one wants to live with the creatures of the forest. One autumn, we started hearing the pitter patter of little paws on our roof at night. It was determined that opossums were climbing the tree next to our house and taking midnight strolls on our roof for whatever satisfaction that was to the feeble opossum mind. My wife and I thought this was charming until alarmingly we started hearing them inside our attic. It is truly amazing how much noise a ten- to twenty-pound creature can make in the middle of the night immediately above your bedroom. We started sleeping in the downstairs room, as the solution to the opossum problem remained unresolved. We subscribe to a monthly pest control service to rid us of ants and other arthropods, but they cowardly maintained their services didn't extend to going face to face with something that could fight back.

Although my self-image is that of a mountain man, my solution to too many problems is to turn to the yellow pages in the phone book. Upon a phone call, C&M Wildlife Removal said they could solve my tribulations with this determined force of nature. Tennessee pioneers would view such a solution with total contempt, but in the artificial world where I dwell, modern solutions are the best I can do. The congenial C&M men arrived and put cages in my attic baited with the all time opossum favorite—peanut butter. Upon their return the next day, they presented me with a very healthy and angry opossum which they took to the woods some distance from homes to release. A few days later another opossum was on the way to join its comrade. Thinking that our furry friends were gone, my wife and I were sitting at the kitchen table when we heard a noise in the hall closet. Cautiously opening the door, I saw two dark eyes looking back at me. The opossum had fallen through the trap door to the attic. My wife decided a day of shopping was in order and happily the kind men from C&M arrived shortly in response to my distress call. They used a stick with a loop on it and lifted one very angry opossum out. My next project was to have the trees next to our house trimmed.

The sheer longevity of this species was brought home to me in a visit to the Dinosaur Walk Museum in Pigeon Forge, one of the many commercial attractions kindly provided for restless children who are less than totally eager for only natural experiences in the wilds of the Smokies. One exhibit shows a small dinosaur eating an opossum with an explanatory note nearby that opossums lived during the full period of the age of dinosaurs and survived whatever destroyed the giant reptiles. Not even the T. rex or the velociraptors could do in the opossum and I always look upon them with respect whether they are in my yard or the wilderness.

There are some apparitions of the deep forest that are rarely seen or may be nonexistent. In many years of hiking I had only a brief glimpse of a fox and never of a wildcat. Some animals that once dwelled in the Smokies are being reintroduced. The park has attempted to introduce otters without much success, but there is a very successful program to bring back elk in the remote Cataloochee Valley, which can only be reached by gravel road and consequentially relatively little tourist traffic.

One of the most controversial mysteries is whether mountain lions or panthers are in the park. Reports of tracks and sightings occur, but there is no definite proof. One friend related how he was camping in the woods and heard a scream that turned his blood cold and which he believed was a mountain lion. After, reading of panther attacks on people in California, I have mixed feelings about being with them overnight in the Smokies. Some animals that lived in the area may never be here again. Amazingly enough, buffalo lived this far east and tourists are startled to see a few fenced in at Cumberland Gap, but one will never again meet them in the Smokies.

In the Smokies, the animal most people are interested in is the bear, and unlike most other animals it may seek human contact or, more specifically, the food that humans have. For the general public, there seem to be two schools of thought about bears. On one side is the Gentle Ben image of a friendly bear, lovable and kindly to all. On the other side is the nightmarish vision of the savage grizzly, ready to rip the limbs off any so foolish as to invade his realm. As for the black bears in the Smokies, neither is quite accurate. Black bears can do real harm if they feel threatened, particularly if there are cubs around, but in the history of the park, only one person has been killed by a bear. However, if one has a realistic approach and treats them with great respect, the physical threat can be kept to a minimum.

As a backpacker, one develops a distinct and unsentimental view of black bears, an insight based on harsh experience. One quickly discovers that a bear is a creature of 300 pounds of cunning with but one mission— to separate the backpacker from his food supply. There are many stories of backpackers on a long trip who lost all their food early to bears and had to endure the rest of the hike in a semi-crazed state of hunger or were reduced to the ignominy of begging for food from fellow backpackers. I guess you can always pack away a sign in your kit that says, "Will carry your backpack for food" in the event such a need arises.

Robert and I never worried excessively about such an event until we were on a hike in the Smokemont area of the park. On this trip, we arrived late and tired at our campsite as we have a tendency to do. After dinner, my assigned task is to hang the bags of food from a suitable tree for the night, hopefully out of reach of the conniving bear and far enough from our tents so we would not be mistakenly identified as potentially tasty morsels. This is an important hiking ritual but one that I had grown increasingly careless with in its proper observation. The general idea is to hang the food bags between two trees with a rope so that the bags are ten feet above the ground and six feet from either tree. In my fatigued state and unable to successfully string a line between two trees I carelessly hung them from only one limb and crawled into my sleeping bag.

The forest at night has many sounds. An active imagination can create more terrors than the mind of a four-year-old wondering what is under his bed. Early in my hiking career I calculated that if I were going to sleep at all at night I would have to ignore all sounds around me, particularly the sounds of an animal near my tent. I always halfheartedly convinced myself that the sounds of padded feet and heavy breathing were those of a raccoon or opossum. On this night, the forest was alive with noise from the little creatures of the woods. The next morning, as I was going to retrieve our food bags, I noticed a lot of debris near our camp. This was strange, because I had not noticed it the night before and most backpackers are very conscientious about litter. Looking up into the tree, I didn't see the food and automatically assumed Robert had already gotten it. "Robert," I politely inquired, "what did you do with the food?" With an indignant tone in his voice, Robert replied, "What do you mean, 'what did I do with the food?' You hung it up last night!" Then the terrible truth dawned— the litter on the ground was what was left of our food supply. All we could find of an edible nature was a tea bag and two boullion cubes. I have often wondered how that bear felt after eating all our freeze-dried foods and then taking a long drink of water from the creek. Do bears get that bloated feeling? Probably not. Happily for us, there were some campers in a site below us who shared their breakfast with us after we told them of our plight. My gratitude for their generosity was somewhat tempered by their subsequent admission that they had heard the bear the night before and had inadvertently driven him towards our campsite. From this up-close-and-personal experience with Euardos americanus, the true knowledge of these canny predators was realized— a large, furry, sentinel forest dweller, dedicated to relieving me of my food, quite capable of outwitting me in his natural home.

When it comes to their survival, animals can be incredibly intelligent and perceptive in ways we do not understand. A National Geographic article described wild geese had to cross land where hunting is permitted in order to enter Yellowstone National Park where hunting is banned. On the approaches to the park the geese would fly low until the moment they crossed into the park, and then would soar high and free into the sky. How they knew the location of the park boundary, a manmade line on the map, is a mystery. A study shows that elephants have a similar awareness. In one location in Africa there are two areas where elephants are protected, but they are separated by an area where they are fair game. No natural features distinguish any of these areas and it was a puzzle to biologists how they were moving from one area to the other. Through the use of radio collars, scientists discovered that the elephants would rapidly traverse from one protected area to another in the depth of night when they were relatively safe and be in the protected areas again when day came. Likewise, any hunter can tell stories of the number of deer they see in the woods the day before hunting season opens but nary a one on the dawn of the opening of the hunt. My encounters with wildlife have brought a tremendous respect for their abilities that might not exist without such pleasant and sometimes scary meetings with them in the wilderness and in my home.

Even our so-called domestic animals have amazing abilities we often do not credit them with, because we believe we have civilized them so they cannot exist without our constant support. One time my wife and I pulled into a rest stop on I-24 in southern Indiana and were puzzled to see a hen with a dozen pullets and one mean rooster parading loose around the area. Thinking they might be some kind of educational exhibit, I inquired from the woman working at the rest stop why they were there. She explained that a truck with chickens on the way to market had stopped and a crate had fallen off the truck and there was a mass escape attempt by the fowl. All were caught except this hen, and the rest stop workers would feed her in her new residence. Later, a man stopped with roosters on his way to cockfighting and said he knew what the hen needed and donated a pugnacious cock-of-the-walk as companion for the lonely hen. The two set up a nest in the woods and the rooster would fearlessly face down all intruders who threatened his flock, including dogs allowed to exercise in the parking lot during a driving break. The woman employee at the rest stop laughed and said, "Our supervisor came by one day and told us the chickens had to go. I told him, 'OK, you do it,' but he wasn't going to take on that rooster." These feisty candidates for Colonel Sanders and the cockfighting ring managed quite well in this unlikely setting with minimum human help.

One winter evening I went out into my backyard and was startled to see a large white rabbit lounging there. It continued to visit us for several days. Upon further investigation I discovered this was Buddy, an escaped pet from a home nearby. It transpired that Buddy had made so many escapes the father told his sons not to bother trying to capture him again and let Buddy go free. I purchased some rabbit food for him and he would run up to me and let me pet him, but he never allow me to pick him up. As he had freedom to come and go as he pleased, he would stay in my yard for a few days and then be gone for weeks at a time. I had not seen him for two months, when driving a few blocks from my home I saw Buddy in a neighbor's yard. Not knowing if Buddy would recognize me after that period of time, I got out of the car and approached him gingerly. Buddy showed no alarm and permitted me to pet him. I was astonished the next morning to see Buddy in our backyard again after his absence of two months. Obviously he remembered me and where I lived. His survival skills were fine-honed and I wondered how long a large slow-of-foot domestic rabbit could live, considering dogs, cars and assorted wildlife that frequented our area. Buddy lived the free life for a year and a half until a neighbor found Buddy dead in his yard. He said Buddy show no signs of a violent conflict and perhaps simply died of old age after living free in his golden years. Once again I am in awe of the animals that share our world.

Night and Day in the Green Cathedrals

In our early years of doing day hikes, the desire arose to reach areas more inaccessible than could be managed between one sunrise and sunset and to more deeply experience the wilderness. These impulses led Robert and me to move beyond mere hiking to the more refined level of backpacking. Spending a night on the trail created new dynamics for our planning and the necessity of more equipment. My first mistake was to buy a backpack far too small for any serious excursions, but that fact was not apparent until much later. For our first overnight trip, we selected a series of trails that would create a loop of some twenty-three miles and include the Laurel Gap shelter for the night so that we wouldn't need a tent. As a good geek, I am fond of drawing lines on a map to record our hiking accomplishments and this hike would be a most impressive addition to the short little spikes that existed so far on my Smokies park map.

This first endeavor was a most ambitious one, as the elevation gain involved was over 4000 feet and we were on trails in the Big Creek area of the North Carolina side where relatively few people venture. The week before we had climbed Mt. Le Conte in one day on a fourteen mile round trip to condition ourselves, but there is a major difference between carrying your lunch for a day trip and what you need for overnight. This two-day loop trip had the advantage of requiring only one car and the additional dividend of not covering the same trail twice. After some easy hiking, the trail started up hill and I felt for the first time the tug of the backpack straps on my shoulders. I was grateful for the modern design of backpacks that places most of the weight on the waist rather than on the shoulders. Nevertheless, the day was hot and the trip was becoming wearying. We came to a little mountain stream that had formed a most inviting pool that called us like the sirens that tempted Ulysses. I had never "skinny dipped" before, but as it was several hours since we had

seen anyone, we felt there would be no problems and besides the etiquette code of the woods is different than flatland standards. The water
was so cold that I only waded in tentatively, and the contrast of my
sweaty overheated body with the frigid water caused me to start hallucinating. I contented myself with going hip deep and was completely
refreshed after that.

Presently, after a seeming eternity of walking up hill, we came to the
Laurel Gap Shelter, our residence for the night. There were only a few
others staying at the shelter including one college student type who
routinely backpacked alone and had an air of superiority towards mortals
less experienced in hiking, such as ourselves. During supper, Robert
pulled two Coke cans from his pack, and the drink was as sweet as any
nectar. Our new acquaintance curled his lip and asked what madness
moved us to bring such a weighty extra item, but that detracted not in the
least from my superb enjoyment of this treat.

As in many learning experiences, neither Robert nor I had adequate
stoves, so our food was only lukewarm, not hot. There are a considerable
variety of hiker stoves on the market, many of which are very tempera-
mental and require meticulous effort to reach that narrow range in which
they will actually operate. After watching people struggle with these,
accompanied by early English oaths, we eventually opted for stoves that
are simplicity itself. Ours is a propane burner with two prongs so that
when the gas tank is attached, it is a three legged affair that gives an
intense flame as long as the gas holds out, which for our purposes is a
week at a time. The importance of hot food and drink in cool weather is
obvious, but even in the most blistering summer days nothing is equal to
a hot cup of tea in the morning and a warm meal at night. That truth
became very apparent on trips when I only ate cold meals. After a hot
country breakfast that warmed our innards in the early morning dews and
mists, we continuously rejoiced in prehistoric man's discovery of fire as
one of the great milestones in human civilization. The normal fastidious-

ness associated with cooking disappears in the forest. While not wanting to be poisoned, the range of tolerance expands greatly and one ignores whatever additional specks happen to be in the boiling water, and food dropped on the ground only needs to have the dirt brushed off. One conclusion in the woods is that sanitation is a much over-rated value and the human body can tolerate an awful lot. If it couldn't, the cave dwellers from whom we descended would have never survived to produce a race of city inhabitants.

Over several backpacking trips we refined what was essential for several nights on the trail. The first consideration is the matter of weight. If you have to carry an item for many miles up a mountain side, it has to be of vital practical use to merit such an honor. The initial thing one discovers is how much water weighs— about eight pounds to the gallon. There is a fine balance here of how much to carry without having an excessive amount. I tend to err on the side of more water, because to run out of it changes any hiking trip into the pain of parched throats and, in extreme cases, a life-threatening encounter with an unforgiving nature. Consequently the most frequent question on the trail of those going in the opposite direction is the next source of water. Signs are not always to be believed, because one friend related how when his group saw a sign that read *Water 500 feet ahead*, they promptly downed the little water they had been so carefully husbanding and then discovered the spring was dry when they got to it. Additionally there is a certain justified paranoia about untreated water in the wild. Robert and I were getting water at the spring at Spence Field when we struck up a conversation with a retired Ohio State math professor and his daughter, a professor at University of North Carolina. The math professor, who looked like an aging Mr. Clean, with muscles bulging under wrinkled skin, was filtering the spring water through one of the purification devices so popular with hikers. I ventured the opinion that this spring water was safe, which was certainly my hope as I had been drinking it in its natural unfiltered state. He congenially responded, "Yes, it probably is, but I don't want to take any chances. Once I was on a week's hike in West Virginia and drank some bad water. A few days into the trip I got so sick I wanted to die, but I couldn't. After that, I always treat my drinking water." Those were certainly words to live by and a consideration of how much treated water from home to carry.

The question of weight extends to the subject of food, another topic of great interest to the backpacker. Some backpackers go to the extreme of taking raisins out of boxes and wrapping the raisins in plastic wrap, so they won't have the extra burden of carrying the boxes. If one is only out for two or three days, it is of moderate importance, but the quantity of food increases exponentially as the planned days on the trail increase. There are satisfactory items that can be purchased in any grocery store such as noodles, oatmeal and soup mixes, but the gourmet hiker wants more variety while keeping down the load to be hauled on one's back. All this leads the backpacker to what is innocently referred to as freeze-dried foods, available at your friendly corner hiking store. It has the great advantage of being light and remaining edible for an indefinite period, but it has the downside of expense and a substantial variation in taste. Some of the products are as appetizing as any prepared food, while others have the taste and consistency of cardboard. Surprisingly, not only backpackers purchase it. One day at work I was discussing the topic with some friends at lunch when one who is not a hiker said he had quite an assortment of it at his house. Puzzled, I asked why, and he explained that as a Mormon his religion required all families to keep a year's supply of food on hand in case of some catastrophe and freeze-dried food was excellent for that purpose.

Several hundred people try to hike the entire Appalachian Trail of 2200 miles each year, or at least significant portions of it. As the whole trail takes about four months of really hoofing it, the question becomes what to do about resupply. A number of ingenious solutions have been developed by the ever-resourceful backpacker. Some have families or friends meet them at a designated time and place where the trail crosses a road. Some mail food packages to themselves at post offices near the trail. The most unique solution is to put supplies in jars and bury them at accessible places and then dig them up along the way. There may be some challenges to this approach, such as finding the exact place after several months and the possibility of bears finding it and indulging in their favorite meal of backpackers' food.

On the first overnight trip we stayed in a shelter, but the question of the proper tent arose for trips where such facilities were not available. In buying a tent, one is faced with many choices. One is size. Do you want to carry your own mansion into the woods or settle for one so small that you can hardly turn over without the danger of rolling over the whole thing? That choice leads directly to the all important question of how much will it weigh and how much will it cost. There is also the question of how easy is it to assemble from a wadded up mess and how simple to quickly return it to a compact parcel. Simplicity is a tremendous virtue because when one arrives exhausted at a campsite with rapidly-approaching dusk, one does not want to have to figure out if pole B goes in socket X or Y like some giant tinker toy set. Likewise, if one has to break camp in a driving rainstorm, it helps if the tent pulls down quickly and does not have a lot of small parts which if lost prevents the tent from being reassembled again under trying circumstances. One vital but easily overlooked specification for a tent is that it can "breathe" so that all the moisture the body naturally generates doesn't condense inside the tent and cause one to awake in a sauna bath. It can come as a great shock to discover just how much water our bodies create and if it is confined where it can't escape, it will drench us. Many tents solve this problem by having a "fly," an extra sheet to put over the tent so that the tent itself can have a top where moisture can escape but the fly will keep out the rain. It also helps if the tent doesn't take up a lot of room on the ground because finding a large level spot in the woods may be an unwelcome challenge.

Of course hikers, being creative types, can come up with novel solutions to the problem of tents and their extra weight. One friend designed his own hammock to take with him. It only required finding two trees a suitable distance apart and very quickly he could settle down for the night. In addition to being light, it also takes advantage of another natural feature, that air is warmer a few feet above the ground. He would cover himself in a tarp in case it rained and, being above ground, not worry about sleeping in a pond as is the case for the unfortunate backpacker who hasn't carefully studied the terrain for where the water will flow if a deluge occurs. Even here there can be drawbacks. He told me that on one trip he hiked late and set up his hammock in total darkness. When dawn came and he could see around, he discovered he had strung his hammock between two trees right on the edge of a cliff. Hikers can be reflective types and he pondered his fate if he had rolled out of the hammock during the night.

Another bizarre solution to the tent problem was described to me by a friend who likes to fish and was in the remote part of the Smokies where Fontana Dam Lake greatly limits access. Night was approaching when he encountered a fellow fisherman and noticed he did not seem to have any gear for an overnight stay. After the usual conversational pleasantries, he inquired of the stranger about his plans for the night. The man chipperly responded, "Oh, I'm a medical doctor and I simply bring some strong sleeping pills. I find a nice place to crawl up on the ground, take my pill and awake refreshed in the morning." Now I consider the person who told me this story to be very trustworthy, but one has to wonder about such a tale, especially coming from a fisherman and their known propensity to stretch the truth. Still, one has to speculate about the good doctor sleeping in the open woods totally drugged-out if a bear comes by or flood waters wash him down to Fontana Dam. (I failed to get the doctor's name in order for me to never use someone with such impaired judgment.)

A final important consideration is the choice of the sleeping bag and what to put under it. Seasoned backpackers often have several, depending on what type of weather is to be encountered. If you camp in the winter, you certainly want one rated for below freezing, but in the summer it would roast you, so a nice selection to fit all occasions is always good. Then there is the question of what to sleep on, and choices range widely from a simple ground mat to a blow up mattress. Before I camped overnight I always had visions of sleeping soundly through the night after a long day of hiking with a heavy pack. What I hadn't realized is how incredibly hard the ground is. My sleep on the forest floor is very fitful no matter what I try or how physically drained I am. Nothing seems to work for me. I tried an inflatable mattress with four separate sections and it didn't seem that much more comfortable; besides, one of the chambers sprang a leak and parts of my body sagged into the vacant area. I am tempted to try my friend's solution of a hammock but have not worked up the courage for that approach.

One great discovery of backpacking is that I can carry on my back all that is necessary for me to live in relative comfort for a week. For all the accoutrements that civilization wants to convince us are essential, most we can live without if the need dictates it or if we want to simplify our lives. Not that I want to live that simply all the time, but for a brief period most of the modern world is nonexistent and I need to rely on myself, my hiking partner, and perhaps others in the woods.

The importance of being the well-prepared backpacker with steady nerves was dramatized to us on one hike. The few weeks in autumn when the leaves have changed to a riot of colors is always a time where one's spirit seems to be uplifted with the pageantry of hues as one hikes the trails. But, unique and unexpected traps wait even in the splendor of blazing foliage. One fall day, Robert and I drove to the "Road to Nowhere" out of Bryson City in North Carolina. This road was to traverse the southern part of the park and connect with the road at Fontana Dam to replace the old road lost beneath the lake created by the dam. It was never completed because of environmental concerns, its tremendous cost, and the desire of many to keep this a remote area.

When we reached the end of the road, we found the leaves were still vibrant at this lower level but had fallen in the higher elevations. We were having trouble locating the start of the trail and searched for several minutes, when a fellow backpacker emerged from the woods. I said, "Let's ask this fellow where the trial he's been on leads."

He was very exceptionally and unexpectedly happy to see us. When we queried him, he told us his unplanned adventure of the last few days. "I started out at Clingmans Dome with the intention of hiking to Fontana Dam over several days. The AT was covered with fallen leaves that made it hard to know where the trail was, and without realizing it I hiked off the trail. I had descended some ways when I recognized I was off the trail and couldn't find it again. I decided to just hike downhill until I came to something. There is no trail where I came out and you are the first people I have seen in three days. When I saw the road, I thought I was hallucinating. Where am I?"

We informed him of his location and we last saw him walking down the road to Bryson City. We had to admire his coolness, because he was hiking cross country in the Smokies, never an easy thing to do, without knowing where he was. If he had been a few hundred yards to the west he would have missed the road and come to the lake with a lot more hiking in his future. He had a tent and plenty of food in his backpack and kept his presence of mind to do logical things to find his way out. Our overnight hike was not nearly as eventful as his autumn journey.

The Smokies are a subtropical forest with only the Pacific Northwest getting more rainfall than these mountains. As I was a sickly child, my mother was always apprehensive about my getting wet. That became an ingrained fear in me. We always hiked with ponchos, but on one early trip the rain was intense for hours with a wind that pelted us with rain in all directions. We soughed through this monsoon for hours and became soaked completely, with the ponchos becoming ineffective against such an onslaught. When we could finally dry out, I was no worse for the wear and I realized that my abhorrence of getting wet was a childhood burden that I had left behind on the trail. Of course it was a warm summer day. Had it been cold to go with it, hypothermia might have been close if our clothes could not keep us warm. This is the great virtue of wool, because it will keep you warm even when wet.

The importance of matching your physical conditioning with the demands of the chosen hike is obvious, but often overlooked. But even being in good shape does not prevent that overpowering tiredness from setting in on a challenging hike, particularly where there is no choice but to persevere until the end of the trail or the campsite comes at long last. During these times, not all thoughts on the trail are of the uplifting type. Indeed, these can reach the darker recesses of the mind. Frequent thoughts when fatigue sets in are: *What am I doing here? What madness caused me to think that trudging up this mountain trail that will never end is going to be fun? Where in the devil is that next spring that the trail guidebook promised for there are only a few drops in my canteen and if we can't find it or if it is dry then it is four miles of parched throat until the next alleged spring. If I can survive this and return with body and soul intact, I will never do this again.*

Now I understand why people who served in the Army demur when I ask them if they want to go hiking despite explanations that this is for fun and the trails are much more scenic than what the Army may have chosen to expose them to. However, once the hike is over and one recalls the good times, the bad quickly fades— until the next time one once again faces the weakness of the body against a steep trail. But one will return again for the joy of the outdoor life.

Certain hikes make it all worthwhile when one can have a peak experience both literally and transcendently. Spring is a season of only a few weeks, and the opportunity must be seized to sample the delights it offers only so briefly. There is a natural garden in the Smokies that would be the envy of any English horticulturist. On the openness of Gregory Bald there grow flame azaleas that have a dazzling variety of colors selected by nature. The shortest way to hike to the Bald is still an eight-mile round trip with a good uphill climb, so only the stronger among the flower loving set will be found at the top. Once there, one is compensated for the effort by seeing one of the great natural displays of flowers in the world. Scattered in this open area are shrubs of flame azaleas each with a distinctive color of red, orange, yellow and pink.

Why the balds exist in the Smokies is uncertain, ranging from natural conditions to the theory they were created by Indians or early settlers. As nature is slowing reclaiming the balds, the latter reason is probable, and the Park Service is working to maintain some of the balds. Whatever the reason, their efforts will preserve this mountaintop garden to reward those who will sacrifice the energy and time to reach a remote part of life that can be seen only through physical exertion.

If you grow up in Florida, the mountains can be your vacation; and after several decades in Tennessee, I have never lost the feeling of awe at a landscape set on its edge. The mountains have a mood that changes by the hour from the freshness of the dawn to the challenge of midday to the pending closure of coming dusk.

The weather changes the landscape from the joy and openness of the cloudless day to the threat of driving rain or snow that dwarfs and overpowers the lonely walker and testifies to one's insignificance in the grand scheme of things. The seasons alter the mood with the renewal of all hope in the spring, the glory of summer with the challenge of heat, the beauty of an all too brief fall with its riot of color, and the soberness of winter. Even on the same trail no two hikes are the same, and this delight and diversity keeps one returning.

Horses, Hunters, and Hikers

Hiking and backpacking opens new horizons to the wonders of nature and usually to the nurture of the spirit, but unfortunately walking on wilderness trails also leads to experiences that were previously unknown. Hiking on the trail is not a total escape from reality and one encounters situations that lead to ill feelings and irrational prejudices that the heart did not heretofore harbor. The joy of hiking is a topic of countless testimonials, but here we must confess to the darker side of our sport that clouds the hiker's mind.

When one treads the mountain trails, it soon becomes very clear that there are others in the woods with different agendas than those in the brotherhood of walkers. The other people in the forest, who, depending on the regulations, have a legal right to pursue other interests. I speak of those who come into the woods on horseback or carrying guns.

Prior to hiking I had a very positive image of horses based on a childhood of watching Western movies and by marveling at their beauty and grace when seen in distant pastures. However, as a hiker, I have acquired an animosity toward these four-legged brutes and their misguided human admirers. The horse is the bane of all hiking trails and the unintentional inflictor of misery upon the hiking population. The reasoning side of my brain says that horses are innocent and that their human riders have as much right to public land as I do. But the problems they create and the interference with MY enjoyment of the wilderness enrages the irrational side of my mind. Early in my hiking experience I was quick to notice the deteriorated quality of some trails and link it to the obvious cause. Not only do their hooves tear up any trail, but it is apparent that all horses suffer from permanent diarrhea of a most unpleasant sort. Thus, any trail where horses have been permitted is often a nasty morass to the hikers who follow and it seriously impacts the pleasure of the wilds. Trails that are frequently used by horses are worn down to the bedrock in many places. One recreation planner told me that horses cause more damage than motorized trail bikes, but planners keep quiet because of the political pressures that would be exerted by the lobby of horse aficionados.

To add insult to injury, the next thing one discovers is that horses have priority on the trail over lesser souls on foot. If you encounter horses on the trail, you are expected to step respectfully off the trail to allow the horse party to pass by in their grandeur. This is always a humiliating and degrading experience that makes the hiker feel like a member of a disadvantaged group that has no protection under the law from an indifferent society. As you stand aside, all hot, gritty and disheveled, the nattily attired riders, with their pristine appearance unaffected by perspiration, inevitably look down their noses at you with a smug and superior air. It provides an insight to how the Aztecs felt when they first saw the mounted Spanish conquistadors ride haughtily by on their mission to destroy entire civilizations.

The problems created by horses, or more accurately, the descendants of Genghis Khan who are mounted on them, can be varied and totally unexpected. Robert and I were on an overnight hike in the North Carolina side of the park, when we crossed a large stream to arrive at our approved campsite. The campsite was the only flat ground in the immediate vicinity suitable for tents and we quickly discovered some troglodytes had recently tied their horses on our officially assigned sleeping plot. The whole vicinity had the consistency of an unkempt barnyard. In attempting to find an alternative site, we forded the stream several times, during the last of which I slipped and fell into the stream and rose from the water to see my favorite hiking stick disappearing in the distance. In total frustration, we decided to give up on our dream of a pleasant overnight outing and drive home.

When you go on hiking trips, you don't take your best car to leave in the woods overnight. Robert's car had a worn wormwheel which required careful driving because it caused the vehicle to weave back and forth on the road. This motion aroused the interest of the local park ranger assigned to monitor for errant drivers and soon the night lit up with flashing lights. As we tried unsuccessfully to come up with the proper vehicle registration and other appropriate documentation I could envision ourselves in the jail at Cherokee. How was I to explain to my wife our presence in the local slammer when we were supposed to be camping deep in the forest that night? Fortunately, the gendarme decided we weren't drunk, merely confused, and let us go.

As a reasonably intelligent and generally unemotional person, I often berate myself for such unbecoming attitudes I have developed through these wayward experiences in what is intended to be a wholesome pastime. In the interest of fairness, I decided to try horseback riding for myself. One year, my wife and I were vacationing in the Grand Teton National Park when we foolishly decided to participate in one of the early morning horse rides with the purpose of having breakfast and enjoying the magnificent surrounding while the horses did all the work. In the wee hours of the dawn, our diverse but valiant group gathered and we were instructed to select a horse. After several queries about which were the most gentle, I settled on one by the name of Sassafras. I do have some knowledge of horses from watching many Western movies in my youth and I knew it was important to let the horse know who is boss. I looked Sassafras in the eye and he looked in mine and in that cosmic connection that occasionally occurs between man and beast, we both knew who was boss: he was. The cowboys in charge arranged us in a single file while they rode on either side, managing the whole affair like some uninspired cattle drive. Sassafras did not have much enthusiasm for his fate of regularly hauling human baggage and demonstrated this lack of interest by going progressively slower as we went along the trail. Consequently the gap between me and the rider in front steadily widened and all my efforts to motivate Sassafras, such as kicking him in the side and yelling appropriate commands, were to no avail. Periodically, a cowboy would come by and give Sassafras a whip on the rear end and he would close the gap, only to slow down again, necessitating the cowboy to repeat the whole process over and over. My ego suffered immensely during the whole ride because of my complete inability to control this vengeful and lazy creature and from the cowboy's look of contempt. The Grand Tetons are beautiful, but I failed to enjoy them on the trip out. When we finally had breakfast, I was already sore and fatigued. The bird that sat on the rim of the vat of flapjack mix with his bottom pointed at the food below didn't detract in the least from my hungrily devouring the vittles that we were given.

Alas, it came time to mount up and start again this human cattle drive. In my dim memory of all those Roy Rogers movies, I recalled that horses are trained to be mounted from only one side. When I asked the proper side, a cowboy curtly told me it was the left side and I correctly mounted without incident. However, one novice mounted on the right side, which is the wrong side from the horse's point of view. I really had no idea this ancient ritual was so important to the horse until this previously docile animal immediately started jumping wildly in an excellent imitation of a rodeo bucking horse. I might have enjoyed this spectacle except that the wild stallion was prancing next to the horse on which my wife was seated and she was looking very threatened by the ordeal. I decided to be the hero and ride to the rescue of my beloved bride and save her in the great tradition of all movies. "Giddyup!" I roared, as I dug my knees into my horse's side. Sassafras, true to his nature, just stood there and I was left powerless to assist my wife. A stalwart cowboy, with courage in his heart and a curse on his lips, waded into the melee and grabbed the horse's reins and brought the situation under control. At least I had the satisfaction of seeing the cowboy berate the crestfallen rider who appeared to be a chief executive officer of some corporation trying to look like the rest of us in his casual attire. At this point, I was so tired of the whole torment that it no longer bothered me on the return trip that the cowboy had to resume his periodic "encouraging" of Sassafras to keep pace as I rode along as some deadweight. However, the next time I went hiking and saw a quagmire of a trail caused by the mounted hordes, I knew the appalling truth of the impact of all this on my soul— I hated horses in the forests and the glens.

In addition to those mounted on horses, there is another group sharing the woods with the walkers, namely hunters, who arrive armed to do battle with creatures I have come only to admire. Each group tends to view the other with a certain degree of suspicion as to their true manhood and ruggedness. They are likely to belong to radically different organizations, such as the hiker who may belong to the American Hiking Society and the hunter to the National Rifle Association. Their paths only cross in the woods and those encounters are of an awkward nature. To protest hunting I would never do as some extreme environmentalists do and follow an armed man into the woods in order to scare off game before he can shoot it. Somehow, angering an armed individual while alone together in the woods does not seem the wisest course of action. I do not have any great philosophical disagreement with hunting, but it is an activity that I could never engage in unless starvation loomed. After all, for the early pioneers, and until recently, the local mountaineers, survival depended considerably on the game they could bag. I am not a native to Tennessee and fear a protest against such an endeavor as hunting would risk revocation of my East Tennessee citizenship. I am always quick to point out to my neighbors that the three greatest Tennesseans of all times were not actually born in Tennessee. I speak, of course of Andrew Jackson, Sam Houston and Elvis Presley, none greater than those three in the Tennessee pantheon. Alas, I digress. In today's world with so many natural predators gone, hunting is necessary to keep us from being overrun with deer and other critters that accommodate themselves so well to our existence. Also, the hunter is just as ardent in preserving wilderness as the hiker.

Nonetheless, it does give me an uneasy feeling to be out enjoying life in green mansions and hear gunshots nearby. My first thought is, *why did I wear that brown jacket today of all days?* However, to give the other side its due, hunters are even less excited about hikers. One hunter friend related the time he rose hours before dawn and made his way through the forest in the dark to his ambush site on a hill above a small valley. There he crouched in the damp undergrowth to await his unwary prey. After several hours of lying still as a cat before a mouse hole, he heard loud human voices coming from below. Two hikers were ambling through the vale, chatting boisterously with one another and enjoying nature. When they had passed, my friend realized that any game would be long gone. Disgusted he stood up and then noticed other disgruntled hunters also standing on both ridges of the valley. Hikers certainly don't contribute to the happiness of hunters, as both are in the woods for very different reasons.

Based on my own brief experience, I have concluded that hunters and hikers don't mix well. On a day hike, Robert and I were in the Joyce Kilmer Memorial Forest which is in a national forest and consequently open to hunters. This area honors the poet who wrote *Trees*, the wonderful ode that begins, "I think that I shall never see/ A poem lovely as a tree." This preserve is a magnificent wilderness of virgin forest that is among the finest in the East, noted for its huge tulip poplar trees. It makes one feel as if one is in a cathedral made by hands far superior to man. On this day, as Robert and I labored up hill, we ran into three men who didn't have the appearance or demeanor of your typical hiker.

After a few moments of pleasantries, one of them inquired seriously, "You fellows see any deer on the trail?"

"No, why do you ask?"

"Well, tomorrow, hunting season opens and we were scouting out the area."

Availing myself of the opportunity to chat with those of the other wilderness faction, I asked, "Do you all hunt any of the wild boars in these parts?"

The hunters replied excitedly, "Oh yeah, we bring in dogs and track them down!"

As we were walking away, I mediated on what would happen if we ever had to contend with such a hunting expedition. Suppose Robert and I were hiking up a trail and hunters and wild animals were coming down the mountain. The first party we would meet might be some very frightened and angry boars with less than charitable feelings about human beings and probably with an inability to distinguish between hunters and hikers. If we got past the boars, the next group would be semi-wild dogs with blood lust in their eyes and mayhem in their hearts. Finally, we would face several heavily-armed men, crazed by the excitement of the chase and agitated by strange noises and movements in the forest and, believe me, Robert and I would have very bizarre movements at this point in time. After reflecting on such a hypothetical scene, we decided not to hike in the national forests during hunting season.

There is one other group in the woods with a lamentable tendency to look down on all the rest of us with a calm and amused feeling of superiority. They are found mainly at the lower elevations and always around water. They call themselves fishermen and dedicate themselves to the annihilation of the edible population of the creeks and rivers, another pastime for which I could never develop any enthusiasm. I learned some about the sport when I served as the personnel officer for a TVA department that included fisheries biologists. Their main concern, at that time, was for some fish called the Snail Darter, but they also had the goal to maintain a varied population of sporting fish in our reservoirs. To do their work they needed to have the knowledge of the types and population of different fish in the lakes, and they conducted what was euphe-mistically called a "fish survey." In their continuing interest of educating uninformed personnel officers, I was invited to participate in one such survey on Norris Lake. The survey involved sealing off an acre-sized cove with nets and then spreading the area with a chemical called rote-none. The effect of this poison is to starve the fish of oxygen, so that they conveniently float to the surface where they are caught to be identified and counted. My part in the exercise was to stand in the front of the boat with a net and sweep them in, a role that made me feel like Captain Ahab looking for the great white whale. The remains of our surveys would be discreetly disposed of away from prying public eyes. In response to my questions about such a procedure, I was assured that there was little damage to the fish population. When the nets were removed, other fish would immediately begin to move into the area, and a week later no one would know that a survey was done. The biologists stated that based on their surveys, most fish die of old age and there is little chance the population will be seriously depleted by sport fishermen. Of course reality is stranger than fiction and when I later related this story to a fisherman friend elsewhere at TVA, he said, "Surely you are putting me on about this one, Dave!" Because of my many strange but true stories, I sometimes lack credibility with others, but later he verified this method of counting fish through other sources.

The attitude of fishermen was best summed up by a psychologist who was working on a project with me and a fellow hiker. He said with some mocking distain, "Yeah, you and Oscar like to be in the woods, but what do you do but get hot and sweaty and irritable while hiking up some ridge line. I, on the other hand, am in the middle of a mountain stream, standing still for hours with the cool waters flowing around me and I know tranquility and a blending with nature that you can never know." His outlook almost made me desire to start fishing, but I hate the thought of cleaning those slimy creatures and I loathe the taste even more. While he had a point, I am still enamored with the idea of walking endless miles to seek new horizons in the mountains. While I must share the woods with others of different interests, we can all rejoice in what is preserved for everyone to enjoy.

Incidents of Travel on the Appalachian Trail

Hikers and backpackers never lack for visions for the great outdoors and one of the prime futurists was Benton MacKaye, who in 1921 proposed an endless trail that he called the Appalachian Trial. Today the AT is a continuous trail of over 2200 miles from Mt. Katahdin in Maine to Springer Mountain in Georgia. Several hundred people have hiked the entire trail and thousands more have enjoyed being on a section of it, often without realizing its extent. It follows the ridgelines and mountain-tops of the grand old mountain range of the east and is reputed to be the longest continuously-marked trail in the world.

Naturally, such a magnificent resource, with its highest point a mere sixty miles from my home, became a focal point of much of my hiking. The trail winds nearly seventy miles across the backbone of the Smokies and this section is the crown jewel of the AT system, (unless you happen to be from New Hampshire and are writing about the trail).

My first trip on the Appalachian Trail was a modest one of six miles to an overlook called the Jumpoff, only a short side trip off the AT. I prevailed on a colleague from New York to go hiking with me despite our very limited experience in walking in the wilderness. The AT from the parking lot at Newfound Gap gradually ascends a mere thousand feet over a stretch of two-and-a-half miles. I have never smoked, but I soon observed its effect for a person in his early twenties. My friend had to take frequent stops, where he breathed rapidly to regain strength. We managed to reach the junction with the Boulevard Trail and found a sign pointing into the woods to our goal. Happily, trails in the Smokies generally are very well marked to assist those with navigational skills considerably less than a Daniel Boone. In 1968, this trail to the Jumpoff was severely overgrown and we found ourselves scrambling uphill through bush and bramble with significant uncertainty as to whether we were on the trail or not, a worrisome situation for two novices in the wilds. I was in the lead and was working my way through the dense vegetation, when I parted some foliage and was stunned to find myself looking at the sky ahead and on the edge of a drop-off of some thousand feet. I concluded that this must be the Jumpoff, as only eternity lay ahead. I recovered from my shock and started reflecting on the consequences if we had crashed pell-mell through the thickets when I heard my companion coming up from below. Surrendering to an ever present perverse sense of humor, I decided not to deprive him of the thrill I had just felt. I casually shuttled off to one side and when he slowly arrived at the point and gazed straight into infinity, I heard, "Oh my soul" or words to that effect.

As far as I know, that may have been the only hiking experience in his life. After we salvaged our composure, and with some debate on whether it should be renamed the Walkoff, we sat at the cliff and quietly absorbed the grandeur before us. The dense forested ridges undulated in rows before us as they had for millions of years and a hawk drifted effortlessly on the air currents surveying the valleys below. Years later, I hiked back to the Jumpoff with Robert, but so many hikers had been there that the heavy undergrowth had been beaten down and anyone could clearly see the fate that lay ahead. Alas, the old thrill was gone, but it was a safer place for the inexperienced.

My next hike on the AT contributed many more valuable lessons about proper preparation and the additional insight that a young marriage will survive a challenging climb, but it was a close call. My wife and I visited Fontana Dam in North Carolina with our eight-month-old daughter. The AT crosses the top of the dam and is the southern start of the trail in the Smokies. My wife and I quite spontaneously decided to hike to Shuckstack fire tower for its promised magnificent views. Now it is only three-and-a-half miles to the top, but it is a 2120 foot elevation gain and I would be carrying our daughter in a packseat on my back. Prior to the hike, we had drunk some of the water out of the canteen with us and my first mistake was to neglect to refill it when there was a chance.

As with so many hikes, the steady uphill climb becomes drudgery very quickly. The trail is unrelenting in its continuous ascent, unrelieved by any significant level section or even a refreshing dip in the trail. Around every turn in the trail one expects to see the welcome sight of that fire tower so the hike will be mercifully ended, but it is not to be. What appears is simply another climb with a taunting turn in the trail in sight, that will in turn lead to another uphill stretch to repeat the process all over again. Guilt soon set in as my young wife struggled up the trail with many observations on the strength of our marriage and I was not feeling so great myself, with our daughter restlessly rocking back and forth in the packseat. Finally we reached the top and we enjoyed the grand view of the lake and dam below us in a triumphal but wearied state, then realized we had to walk down; and as we had drunk all the water, it would be a thirsty descent.

The descent has challenges of its own, for many different muscles are used than in the ascent. The constant pounding of stepping downhill can become excruciating, especially on the knees, as the endless trail repeats itself in reverse. Fortunately, our marriage survived intact and our hiking as a couple continued, albeit with a little more planning in the future. After this hike, I had considerable aches in my legs that caused me to limp around for several days. I was still in my twenties then, but the unfamiliar exercise had exacted its toll. Interestingly, following this sojourn, I never had muscle aches, even though I might get very tired. Apparently the body adjusted to this form of physical activity.

Several years later I faced the descent down Shuckstack Mountain again under very different circumstances, but not less trying. Robert and

I faced a fourteen-mile hike to our car at Fontana Dam. We were on a three-day hike that started at the dam, where we had hired someone to take us across the lake by boat and drop us off at the head of Hazel Creek. The first day was pleasant enough— we enjoyed a campsite next to the creek and a refreshing swim in its cool swift waters in the complete solitude that this side of the park often offers. The next day was a long and grueling hike of six-and-a-half miles up Jenkins Ridge to the shelter at Spence Field. Perhaps the only thing worse than a continuous uphill trail is one that goes up and subsequently dips into a valley and then climbs up again to regain the elevation that was so strenuously acquired earlier. Jenkins Ridge trail has three such dips and lives in agony in our memory forever.

We had not planned to stay at Spence Field but to go on to Russell Field three more miles down the Appalachian Trail. But because of our exhaustion, we made the decision to stay at Spence Field and were fated to have our anxious night there.

The nest morning, we had regrets that we now had a fourteen-mile hike ahead of us on the AT. Robert and I are never very fast hikers, particularly with a fully-loaded backpack, and when we finally arrived at Shuckstack fire tower the sun was fast disappearing. We decided not to go up the fire tower for its views, as a certain desperation was occurring due to the lateness of the hour. Some consideration was given to simply pitching our tents and spending the night on the trail, but we were stayed from this stratagem by the knowledge that our wives were expecting us that evening and if we did not appear, the ensuing concern might prohibit us from future overnight excursions in the woods. With little choice we plunged on down Shuckstack in the twilight that was soon darkness. We had flashlights but we discovered that they were almost useless, as their feeble beams seemed to be swallowed up in all-encompassing shadows, so we couldn't even tell where the trail was. Finally, we just walked in the gloom, trying to pick out the wide spaces between the trees on the assumption that in that gap was the trail. Assuming we didn't walk off a cliff, the worst outcome would be to become lost and forced to spend the night in the woods. The lights of Fontana Dam below us were visible periodically and gave us hope.

At last we arrived at the dam but still faced another mile at midnight walking to the marina where our car was parked. Sometimes stalwartness is trumped by fatigue and one resorts to measures disdained in more rested times. Fontana is a TVA dam, and shortly after crossing the dam two TVA public safety officers pulled up to check us out. Encountering hikers is a routine occurrence for them and when we told them our destination they only wished us well despite my secret wish that they would give us a ride to our car. As a TVA employee who drove a van with their manager as one of my passengers, I cunningly enquired, "Oh, by the way, I am a TVA employee, and Captain Track rides in my van. Do you know him?" The response was immediate, "Yeah, he's our big boss. Would you like a ride to your car?" I am sure I violated some government rule doing that, but exhaustion sometimes brings out the sinister side of all of us. There is joy and pain in hiking, but there are also memories that last long after the weariness is gone and that trip was the stuff of many a yarn.

Robert and I had made it our goal to hike all the Appalachian Trail in the Smokies, but to do it in sections. To complete another segment, we went out on a fine autumn weekend to hike from Newfound Gap to Cosby, a distance of twenty-five miles. After doing the shuffle of parking a car at Cosby and then driving around to Newfound Gap, we were ready for the ten miles of the first day with our night's destination at Pecks Corner Shelter. Early on the trail, three young muscular guys rapidly overtook us heading in the same direction. We found out they were soldiers on leave, had been a couple days on the trail. We were all heading to the same shelter for the night. However, after we told them of our goal, they viewed us with considerable skepticism and said, "Well, we will see you there," with a tone of distain. The hike along the AT that day was wonderful, enjoying the multitude of autumn foliage and leaving the many day hikers behind after we passed Charlies Bunion four miles out.

Robert and I had a leisurely stroll, at least as leisurely as is possible with a loaded backpack, so it was late in the day when we arrived at the shelter. The only other occupants were our three soldiers, who expressed amazement that we had made it. It is magnificent to be in the wilderness, but there is no need to be totally primeval about our absence from civilization, for we also value fine dining when we can. For the first day out, it was our practice to take a frozen round steak surrounded by bacon for the evening meal. By the time we were ready to cook, the steaks would be thawed.

In discussing food with our new friends at the shelter we found out they were surviving on a diet of oatmeal for several days, which was obviously not improving their spirits judging by the bickering between them. They had already eaten their puny fare for dinner. Being hungry, we quickly proceeded to fry our steaks and the baked potatoes we also brought along for the occasion. We were oblivious to the impact on our temporary companions of this simple act of preparing a fine cuisine with succulent aromas wafting about our camp site. The largest of the soldiers was named Kirby and he had apparently eaten well in his life. He had a forlorn look in his face as he surveyed our efforts and said wishfully, "Those steaks sure smell good." With some guilt we ate our steaks and potatoes under Kirby's watchful eyes.

The next morning the soldiers were up early and eating their oatmeal when Robert and I once again tucked into a hearty breakfast to greet the morning sun and a hard day on the trail. For our standard morning meal Robert would bring fresh eggs in a strong plastic carton to keep them from being crushed, and I would bring a couple cans of Vienna sausages. Once again the campsite was filled with a tantalizing bouquet, this time of a country breakfast and the none-too-subtle observation from Kirby,

"Those eggs and sausages sure smell good." We were thankful that Kirby was not the violent type, but one can never be certain of what a steady diet of oatmeal may do to even a balanced person after several days on the trail.

The second day's hike was enjoyable until it was time to descend. At 5800 feet we left the AT to follow the Snake Den Mountain Trail that in five miles would take us down 3400 feet to where our car was parked at the Cosby campground. This trail is a killer on the knees, as it drops constantly. On occasion we could see down to the base of the mountain through the trees, and the end seemed impossibly far away beneath us. I would go as long as I could and finally say, "Robert, let's take a break here," and drop my pack and collapse spread-eagle on the ground and wonder if this is where my life would end. Finally the most welcome sight in all of hiking occurred when the car came into view.

On another trip we labored down the Snake Den Mountain Trail and arrived at a designated campsite in midday. Normally we didn't pay much attention to other campers and their accouterments, but this camp had an eerie feel about it. It was in considerable disarray even for a camping site, with items scattered about wildly and no one around. There was a sense of evil and foreboding, as if coming upon some dark crime scene. We continued down the trail and subsequently met a park ranger coming up the trail. When we reported to him our observations about the campsite, he said, "Yes I know all about it and I am coming up to get the gear. A family was in the campsite and all night they were harassed by a bear. At the first light they cleared out leaving everything behind." One can only guess if they ever took up backpacking again.

Robert and I had set our goal to hike the 68 miles of the AT in the park, which we did in five different hikes, but more daring souls than ourselves did it in record time. In an account in our local newspaper, Jerry Eddlemon, a young graduate student, ran the whole length in under twenty-six hours, a trip that most backpackers would take six or seven days to do. He would have done it in less time except for being delayed by encounters with bears and wild hogs. As with all records, this one may have been broken by others in superb shape and who can run the trail at night.

To do all of the AT in the park, four of our sections required overnight trips, but we did one segment as a day hike. The AT from Newfound Gap to Clingmans Dome is parallel to a road in order for the public to access the highest point in the park. After driving up this road, there is a half-mile paved trail to the summit, so even the general public must abandon its cars and exert some energy if they want to be on top of the Smokies. At the high point is an observation tower that affords a magnificent view of the area. When winter comes the road to the Dome is closed, as it becomes too dangerous to drive with possible snow and ice at any time.

Robert and I decided to hike this section in late November so we wouldn't be hearing cars constantly on the road near the trail, and when we did reach the top we would have a solitary experience that would be impossible when the road was open and there were hordes of tourists about. I drove us in my old Buick Century, which was a powerful automobile. But since it does not have front wheel drive, it was lacking in control on ice and snow. On the way to Newfound Gap in the early morning, we came to a section that in the winter is in almost constant shade and where water crosses the road. At this time of day, the water had all turned to ice, but I was unaware of it until we were in the middle of its treacherous grip. Suddenly the car was spinning in the road and I watched helplessly as I saw before us the looming downhill slope. Then we spun around to face the bluff where the road had been cut; then we observed the road up hill, and the 360 degree process all over again. Somewhere in the back of my mind was the technique of Yankee drivers to turn the wheel into the spin, but I was not sure if I wanted to as there were at least two directions I did not want to proceed in afterwards.

Fortunately no other cars were on the road, so we could play out our ballet without colliding with someone else. Finally the car started sliding off the road to the downhill side and in my passive resignation to my fate, I could only hope we wouldn't go too far down the hill before trees stopped this massive vehicle that now had a mind of its own. At the last minute the car came to a dry spot and the brakes caught hold a few feet before we tumbled down the side. After a few minutes to regain our composure we decided to go on.

As we left Newfound Gap, we were rewarded by walking in a lightly snow-covered wilderness whose quietude would be marred if cars were passing nearby. We sauntered up the eight miles to the top as the winter day started to end, but we had planned to walk back on the road so that hiking in the dark would not be a problem on this trip. We came to the top and ambled up the familiar curling ramp to the top of the overlook structure. There we enjoyed the view in a peacefulness seldom known at this popular destination. Lost in our thoughts, a faint noise of a motor vehicle caught our ears and steadily grew louder. How is this possible as the road is closed and it is a half mile to the parking lot in any event? Then a four-wheel ATV came into view driven by two barbarians who parked at the base of the tower. We tried to be social with them and asked them how they did it with the road closed. They blithely admitted they drove around the barriers at the base of the road and the poles at the start of the trail. We left them and descended the paved trail to the parking lot, brooding about our lost solitude in this mechanized world with the louts who operate them. When we arrived at the parking lot, our hearts leaped with joy as we saw a park ranger pull up in a car. In the best tradition of Benedict Arnold, we rushed over to him and reported the ATV at the top. This steadfast lawman relied, "Yes, I knew they went up the road because I saw the tire tracks in the snow going around the barricade. If they had stopped here in the parking lot I was only going to give them a fine, but as they drove it up the trail I am going to book them. I'll wait here until they come down."

With a song in our heart knowing that justice would prevail we started down the road in the dimming light. After a short time, around the bend came the two law breakers on their ATV with the park ranger in his car right behind them. We hypocritically smiled and waved to them as they disappeared to face the just vengeance of the law for violating this wilderness. After several hours of walking the road, we came to New-found Gap and gingerly drove our car down the mountain, ever mindful of the earlier spin at the icy patch.

My favorite section of the AT in the park is the section from Spence Field to Thunderhead Mountain that for a mile and a half is almost entirely open rocky terrain and grassy meadows. I first came to this part when we did the twenty-three mile trip from Newfound Gap to Cades Cove as part of our project to hike all of the AT in the park, and I fell in love with it immediately. In the middle of this section is Rocky Top, a peak dear to all Tennesseans because of the song of that name that particularly stirs those with the orange blood of the University of Tennessee in them. It is a natural rock platform with an unobstructed view that to me is the finest in the park. As the shortest way to reach this section is a five mile trail from Cades Cove to Spence Field with a 2500-foot elevation gain, it is guaranteed never to be very crowded unless a large group is coming through. Generally one has the solitude to enjoy this view at the top of the world. I have returned to it several times in all seasons, and it was the longest hike my wife walked so she, too, could have the honor of standing at Rocky Top, Tennessee. (It is also partly in North Carolina, but we will ignore that part for a good story.)

On one winter day, Robert and I hiked to Rocky Top to see the section in the snow. When we got to Spence Field I was so hot from the exertion of the uphill hike that I was walking through the snow in a T-shirt. This was a bizarre feeling, as it was wintry enough for the snow to be there, but I was so hot it seemed I was only walking through white powder. Finally, I reached my hand down into the snow for the unnecessary confirmation that it was indeed cold. No matter how hot you are in such conditions, when you take a snack break, the reality of where you are quickly asserts itself and the chill you feel requires donning the down jacket. The view from Rocky Top was once again rewarding, but this time to see the winter barrenness of the park around us. With the foliage gone, we could see the triangle patch of Spence Field most clearly in the distance below us.

Robert and I completed all the AT in the park, and it remains our most rewarding experience in our hiking career. Not all experience this joy, as weather can be everything, particularly if you are unable to enjoy the splendor of the views this apex of the AT offers. In his book, *A Walk in the Woods*, about hiking parts of the AT, Bill Bryson only briefly relates hiking the southern half of the AT in the Smokies with the curt observation that it was all in the fog and rain and he and his buddy abandoned the effort half way through and got a ride to Gatlinburg in order to pick up the AT much further along. It is sad that miserable weather can hide from those who come only once to the Smokies the glories it has to offer, but it is the high rainfall that makes it what it is, the finest wilderness in the Eastern United States.

After Robert and I had hiked the AT in the park, we decided to sample some of the trail outside the park by going forty-six miles from Allen Gap to Davenport Gap. Once away from the park for an overnight hike, there is always an important concern about how to handle the car issue, more specifically where to safely park our vehicles for several days. Our starting point of Allen Gap is fourteen miles above Hot Springs, North Carolina, and a week before the hike I drove up to the area to scout out the situation. I discovered that where the AT crossed the highway at the Tennessee/North Carolina border was a lonely spot. There was only one little general store at that place and, as it was in the middle of the national forest, not many people lived around it. The only discernible reason for the general store to be at that location is that it is to be the first place people from Tennessee could drive to buy cheaper cigarettes, because North Carolina tobacco tax is so much less. The store had a large parking area and I went in to get permission to leave my car for several days. The apathetic woman clerk was indifferent to my parking there but pointed out they were closed at night. I inquired about how safe my car would be in this remote section of the road and she reflected for a moment and said, "Well, I guess it depends who comes along." I failed to find fault in that logic, but it gave me a certain pause and I determined that some other arrangement would be more desirable. I drove to Hot Springs and made inquires at the local gas station and was informed that Old Joe at the fire station would shuttle hikers for a modest fee and we could park our car next to the fire hall.

Suitable arrangements were made with Old Joe to take us to our starting point, and when the day arrived he was true to his word. We had a congenial conversation with him on our trip as he made general observations about backpackers. In the course of hiking this section outside the park we discovered significant differences from the AT in the park. There are few day hikers on the trail, except around an easily-accessible spot such as the grassy meadow at Max Patch, but one en-counters many overnight hikers out for long stretches. Another major difference is the less wild nature of the forest, because of having more extensive human use in the recent past. Some of the AT is on lands close to farmhouses, so the isolated wilderness experience is not present. The feeling of still being part of civilization was inescapable.

On the second day of the hike we came again to Hot Springs to spend the night at the hostel for backpackers run by Jesuits, although we never did see anyone who appeared to be in charge. Not being true purists in the wilderness experience, we borrowed our car from the fire station parking space and had our trail dinner at the local McDonalds.

That night at the hostel we distressingly discovered that our bunks were in a room to be shared with Boy Scouts from St. Louis. Worse still, the scoutmaster wasn't going to be in our room. As I turned in for the night amid considerable commotion I resigned myself to a rather sleepless night. Suddenly, the large bulk of the scoutmaster appeared in the doorway, and he screamed at the top of his voice in the finest tradition of a drill sergeant, "I don't want to hear a single sound from any of you or you all are going to be dead meat!" and the lights went out. It was a full five minutes before I dared to move a muscle. After a night of blissful sleep I concluded it wasn't all that bad to be around Scouts if they were under firm control. Sadly this hostel is now defunct.

The rest of the trip was uneventful, and we were blessed occasionally with spectacular views. It did bring the realization that the quality of the AT varied greatly at different locations, with some being near pristine wilderness and others handicapped by proximity of human habitation and the paucity of virgin forests. If there was any desire to hike all the AT— which was quite out of the question being married with children and with an employer who would take a dim view of a four-month absence— this impulse to complete the whole length in one go was quailed by the realization that a considerable amount of the time I would be trudging through mundane woods when I had been bred with the high standards of the national park.

A Soccer Interlude

As satisfying as hiking and backpacking became in my life, there was a lingering curiosity— an unfulfilled desire— to know what it would be like to be part of a true team sport. Because of the limited physical activities in my youth due to my heart condition, I am totally lacking in sports skills such as the coordination required for any type of ball handling or hitting. Consequently, in my adult years I avoided recreational sports such as softball or basketball to save myself embarrassment and spare my teammates exasperation with me. There seemed little way that I could be in a team sport where my deficiencies would not be very obvious.

However, the opportunity did arise to test my mettle on the playing field. My youngest daughter was on a soccer team, so I was presented with the opportunity to watch several matches and learning a little about a game that before had only elicited typical American indifference. During this time, a good friend came to me and said "Dave, we are organizing a soccer team and you should join." When I demurred with the reason that I had no skills in the game, he replied, "No one else will have soccer skills either." He explained that the recreational league would consist of men over thirty and women over eighteen, with a minimum of five women on the field at any one time. There would be very liberal substitution, so you didn't have to be on the field longer than you wanted. It was designed to be a fun type of league. I was told that there were other leagues for those who wanted to seriously compete in the game. After thinking about it, I agreed, reasoning that no American man over thirty would have any soccer skills, so I would not be conspicuous in my inadequacies.

Being then in my forties, I was one of the older players. Due to lack of speed and endurance, I usually played in the defensive position. I did learn the rudiments of playing the game and could do reasonably well in impeding threats in my general area by kicking the ball back up field, or, if necessary, out of bounds. The value of teamwork rather than trying to be the star player quickly became obvious. I was impressed with the long periods of inactivity while I causally watched action elsewhere on the field and then the suddenly very intense activity as I desperately scrambled when the ball and several hostile players materialized in my area. My soccer skills were not great, but I did not feel totally out of place, receiving frequent encouragement from my associates in this fun endeavor.

We were fortunate to have Stan as a goalie. Stan was my hero. He was lankly six-footer with absolutely no fear. He would charge with a scream to make a Viking proud whenever the ball threatened our goal and he would lunge at the ball no matter the risk of getting kicked by incoming players. He kept us in many a game; especially as I was one of the last lines of defense before he was called on to perform his duties. Over time, I came to appreciate the camaraderie, the working together for a common purpose, and "the thrill of victory and the agony of defeat" as a "team player" Our team liked to seriously party, which was also outside my normal mode, so this also was a part of the sport experience that I had never had before.

One statement needs to be qualified. This was to be a "fun" league and not to be intensively competitive, but the winning instinct will soon assert itself no matter how lame or slow of foot the participants. It occurred to all teams in the league simultaneously how to obtain that winning edge, that extra margin that feeds the primeval desire for victory, that urge to emerge superior over lesser mortals. It is generally true that Americans over thirty won't have any soccer skills, but as in any urban area, there are the foreign-born among us, and many of them have played soccer since they were old enough to chase a ball. Without any outside or official encouragement, our teams embraced equal opportunity for all nationalities with a vengeance. We started our team with a forward who had grown up in Poland and who was almost unstoppable if he had the ball and the only obstacle between him and goal was some unfortunate American learning how to be goalie. I was amazed how many games we won that first year.

When in public, one becomes quickly very alert for a foreign accent. A casual conversation would be started, until one cleared his voice, and popped the critical question, "Oh, by the way, have you ever played soccer?" Our Polish player moved away after the first year, but we had a Columbian and an Iranian on the team for several seasons. The main cultural problem arose in practice where they would approach our training with an intense seriousness of purpose that they found lacking in us. Let's party! On one memorable day a team member showed up to excitedly announce the news that she had found an Argentine who would join our team. We couldn't have been more thrilled if it had been Diego Maradona himself. Indeed our Argentine player was a terror on the field, but for only fifteen minutes or so, for alas, a lifetime of smoking imposed severe limits on him.

All teams recruited foreign players, so as a defensive back I had to face these talented individuals. In one game, a short, stocky, swarthy person, older than I was, lined up against me. As I surveyed him, I thought that this guy shouldn't be hard to cover. I wondered why they had him as a forward. Then the ball came our way and almost before I could move a muscle he had the ball, zipped around me and was headed unimpeded for the goal. All I could do was yell, "Watch out Stan, here he comes." After he slammed the ball into the back of the net his other team members yelled, "Way to go, Benito!" I figured Benito had been playing soccer a lot longer than I had.

Some teams with less honor than ourselves would use any means to get the winning edge, or at least they thought of a strategy before we did. One team recruited women from the University of Tennessee soccer team. On this occasion, I was sizing up the young woman in front of me, when I discovered just how hard it is for a forty-something guy to chase down a fit twenty-year-old Amazon. During the game, Stan was punting the ball when it came in our direction. Before I could do anything, she turned around and gave a mighty kick to the ball and blasted it into the goal beyond Stan's outstretched hands. This left me to brood about the injustices of facing such talent and reflect on the lack of such humiliations on the hiking trail.

One amazing thing to me was the number of injuries that occurred during the normal course of play. We were not conceived as a highly competitive league, but many people went down, often through no contact such as with a twisted knee. The attrition rate was astounding. One woman was just standing in position when an opposing player about ten feet away kicked the ball and it hit her on the wrist and fractured it. She had to drop out from that mishap. There was a certain roughness in play that I had not expected. I was standing nonchalantly in my usual defensive role when the ball came soaring towards me followed closely by an angry mob of our players and theirs. In the split second that I had, I decided the safest course was to kick it out of bounds. I watched with satisfaction as the ball went out of harm's way when suddenly the ground came rushing up at me, the result of a late arriving opponent. As I lay sprawled on the muddy ground, I thought at least we will get a penalty out of it. While I slowly got up, I heard the referee say, "No penalty, he was going for the ball." No penalty! The ball was gone when I was flattened. However it appeared useless to argue. Later, in the game, I was knocked down again. After those two incidents, I reflected in wonder how anyone manages to play American football where tackling is expected and encounters with the hard surface are routine. After two knockdowns, I was ready to call it a day and go home.

The intensity on the field of play was new to me; far more passion was expended than in the normal range of life. Smalltalk between opposing players did not appear to be proper etiquette. When action was elsewhere I would spend long minutes staring at the forward in front of me. It seemed strange not to engage in a friendly conversation, but I discovered the ethics of competitiveness did not permit such niceties. It was also a great shock to discover a kind and gentle friend off the field would scream rudely in my face on the field if I happened to be playing out of position. The social environment on the field was more like a work situation where when things have gone wrong the search is on for a scapegoat. Emotions displayed on the field would also be unacceptable in my normal subdued communal life. On one occasion, I was in a large melee in front of our goal, trying to assist Stan, when the other team scored, and the primal yell of triumph from one of the opposing players seemed like the bellow of a caveman who had just brought down a woolly mammoth. Indeed, my overall experience gave me a new insight into human life that I lacked from the perspective of the viewing stands or the pleasant encounters with others on the hiking trail.

Hiking and backpacking generally have limited ego involvement. I am proud when we complete a hike and reach our goal and more significantly return from it, but it is no disgrace not to finish a planned hike because of unexpected conditions such as excessive ice on the trail or physical discomfort. Indeed sometimes prematurely ending a hike can be a virtue and a source of praise from others for your wisdom. Organized sports are otherwise. The goal of winning becomes all and you have an empty feeling even if you contributed all you could, or worse, were a cause of the defeat. In any given league there is only one winner; the rest walk away with a less than complete feeling. A wise coach, perhaps, more candid or perceptive than most, once said, "Sports is learning how to deal with failure." As the teams I was on did not place first in any season, I left my foray into this area with many good feelings but also sadness that does not linger over me for any of my hiking experiences.

It would be fitting if I could provide a Hollywood ending to this account and describe the time I scored a goal. Alas, dear readers, it is not so. On one of the few occasions I was allowed to play forward, I was in a mob chasing the ball toward the goal when an opponent tapped the ball back to his goalie. On the theory that anything could happen, I charged after the ball and the goalie, in his dive for the ball, slipped and only batted the ball and it came careening to me with an open net looming. An inner voice said dribble it gently forward for the shot, but in my eagerness I gave a hard kick and it went off the side of my foot and missed the goal by a few feet. That image of my sole opportunity to score a goal lingers yet. I learned that reality is an unwelcome intruder on the playing field where one seeks to escape into the fantasy of glory.

During the course of events, I was asked if I would referee in the children's soccer league. That seemed like a good idea at the time, as I could learn the rules better and help young people build character. After the appropriate training course, I was ready to go. As I was a novice, I started out with the beginning league where six year olds were playing for the first time. All things considered, I was amazed at how well they understood what was expected of them, even at the basic level. They did know the purpose of scoring and had a reasonable grasp of the rules, although the temptation to pick up the ball was great. Refereeing this group, I had the additional advantage that most parents do not know the rules of soccer, which greatly reduced the abusive language often directed at referees. However, there were certain issues at that young age.

In our very first game of the season I gathered the diminutive team captains in the middle of the field and explained to one, "All right, you are the visiting team and you get to make the call on the coin toss that decides who gets the ball first. When I throw this coin in the air, you say, 'heads' or 'tails'." I flipped the coin up and the steward little captain said, "Heads or tails." No, what I mean is, you say 'Heads OR tails'. Next coin toss, he said "Heads OR tails." As this could go on for some time, I said to him, "You want heads, don't you?" After his nod, I tossed the coin and we began the game.

At this level a prime concern is to make sure no one gets hurt. If I noticed a shoelace untied, I would stop the game and tie the child's shoe myself as the fastest way to get on with the event. One of the children concluded that was an official duty of the referee, and during a break he held up his foot and said, "Ref, my shoe is untied."

Sometimes, it is difficult to decide how to apply the rules. In one case, a team lost track of which direction they were supposed to go in and made a determined assault on their own goal with the ball. The opposing team just stood and watched and I was trying to think if there were any rules against scoring in your own goal. Fortunately, one little tyke realized the error and ran around among his teammates yelling, "We are going the wrong way" and managed to kick it out of bounds.

Later I was advanced to refereeing older children. By then both the players and the parents knew the rules, which was unfortunate from my viewpoint because of the unkind remarks that ensued. I discovered how difficult refereeing can be. Perhaps if I had years of soccer experience it would be easier, but during play I would see something happen and try to figure out if a foul had been committed. As action is continuous, I had only a brief second to decide before play moved on down the field and I tried not to be influenced by the shouted advice of coaches and parents. It is said you shouldn't judge others until you walk in their shoes, and I vowed to be far less critical of referees in the future. My career in refereeing was for only two seasons. At that time in my work life, I had a job in personnel work where I was called on to make decisions that frequently were unpopular with my fellow employees. I decided that I didn't need to be criticized about things that are supposed to be fun, and I gave it up.

All in all, playing soccer was a very fulfilling endeavor for me. It gave me a glimpse into team sport that I had lacked, with the feeling of being "this band of brothers," and with a new perspective on winning and losing. Living in a region where college football is a near religion (and I am one of its devotees), I came away with the feeling that players and coaches may have a better attitude than fans who criticize from afar. After all, if you do all you can and lose, that does not indicate a moral or social failure. You are not a lesser human being; you simply did not win that day. There are two determined teams on the field and one has to lose. However, as it is important to experience all that life has to offer, I have this time for my memory and a sense of fulfillment that once in my life I was a part of a sports team. Now back to the important activity of hiking and backpacking where my true identity lies.

Wyoming and the Wild West

Many people like to spend their vacations in the same place every year, based on the idea that a vacation is a time to rest and renew oneself and to be away from the test of the unfamiliar. That is all well and good, but over the years I have taken the philosophy that the first day back at work should seem more like the real vacation than the rigors that can be encountered on a volunteer basis. Many a Monday morning after the travails of the previous week's vacation, I have sat at my desk barely able to move and thankful that we survived uncertain circumstances. Fortunately my wife shares and/or tolerates my outlook and while my children had little choice in the matter they took the same approach in their adult life.

For those born and raised in the effete East, the rugged virtues of the West hold an almost mystical appeal. Of course that appeal could be based on an excessive number of Western movies and TV series so prevalent when I was growing up, but there is always hope of a reality behind the fantasy of Hollywood. As a hiker, it was constantly a goal to walk in this western nirvana at some point in life, to test myself in the land of Roy Rogers and John Wayne and to see the incredible beauty and the sheer wildness of the open spaces. The woman of my dreams is from Missouri, a state I had never been to before, but I now have logged some fifty trips there that put me closer to the West I longed to see.

Our first trip "out west" was to Rocky Mountains National Park, but I had limited prospects of hiking since my wife was four months pregnant. Nevertheless, the overwhelming grandeur of that park, with a road that goes to 12,000 feet, was awe inspiring. To be above the tree line for the first time and see the rugged, almost desolate terrain of rocks, peaks and withered alpine growth was to experience the world in its earliest creation. We did make a short hike to stand before Emerald Lake with its pristine blue water and mountains soaring above it. This initial encounter only fueled the desire to hike once again in an environment so alien to my early imprinting.

Some years later, my wife and I vacationed in Jackson Hole, Wyoming, and did some short hikes in the national parks of the Grand Teton and Yellowstone, two parks next to each other but amazingly different in character. The Grand Teton Mountains soar above a flat valley in an abruptness that speaks of a violent geological past. With several lakes in front reflecting their glory, the range stands as an inviting bulwark for further exploration. We took the boat across Jenny Lake and hiked into the seclusion of Cascade Canyon. After a brief climb to the aptly named Inspiration Point, we walked for several miles in the narrow canyon with mountains towering a mile above us that seemed youthfully energetic with the frequent waterfalls gushing down their sides. As I hiked this trail I thought that surely this was the most beautiful place on earth.

The contrast of Yellowstone could not be more jarring with terrain that, while attractive, did not have the overpowering beauty of the Tetons. But here the earth is alive like no other place with its ten thousand thermal features. We hiked the Lower Geyser Basin with its countless thermal features that created nervousness in a mist of a moving and boiling earth with frequent unexpected eruptions of mud or steam next to the precarious wooden-planked path that you walk on and cling to for safety. To hike here is to see the world still being created with a threatening power to consume you if you make one false step, unlike the tranquility I seek in nature. As I seek constant variety in hiking, nothing could give me more of that than this terrain changing before my eyes.

Years later, Robert and I went to the area equipped for backpacking and determined to pit ourselves against the western wilderness. In order to maximize the brevity of time, one wants to select the best trails for the area. This entails a certain amount of research prior to departure. A week before our leaving I came across the Sierra Club guide to the Wind River

Mountains, which I had never heard of before, and I discovered that it was a remote area the size of Connecticut made up of three national forests and an Indian reservation. While it does not contain the highest peaks in the area, it is unique in the vastness of the expanse and the beauty of its mountains and lakes, and we quickly added it to our growing itinerary of desirable hiking areas. Flying into Wyoming, our plane passed directly over it and some comprehension of its immensity could be gained.

We made the Wind River our first target. Driving to our jumping off point of Big Sandy Campground, we drove miles on a dirt road in the flat barrenness of scrubland that is Wyoming away from mountains, and I understood why the population of this state is the same as our home county. As we saw few cars, I excitedly told Robert, "We will be hiking in a pristine wilderness without anyone else around," an observation soon disproved when we got to the parking lot and saw several hundred cars, including one from our Knox County, Tennessee. But the area is so enormous that one is alone most of the time.

Robert and I were use to hiking in the Eastern forests, so to hike in the Rockies was a totally different experience in many unforeseen ways. In the east, we would hike in the deep forest almost continuously with only occasionally being rewarded with a view. Also, the mountains tend to be feminine, with few sharp edges except rarely such as Grandfather Mountain in North Carolina. Here in Wind River we were almost constantly in the open, with new vistas at almost every step. The feeling generated is opposite from the East. In the Smokies you have a feeling of enclosure in the wilderness as if you are its prisoner, for it to do with you as it wants. In the West, the sheer continuous openness creates a heady feeling of freedom and expansiveness, as if your horizons are unlimited and there is no control on where you can go and what you can do. Perhaps herein lies some of the differences between the mentality of the Easterners and Westerners. Another major distinction is the availability of water in the Western mountains. On the high trails in East, water is a constant concern, sometimes to the point of obsession. But in the mountains of the west, where snow lingers all year round and conveniently melts on a constant basis, water is plentiful. For beauty there are frequent meadows covered with wildflowers that appear to be deliberately planted but are wild, with names like Indian Paintbrush and Shooting Stars.

We hiked the Big Sandy Trail to Big Sandy Lake where we camped for the night. Other campers were around, but considerate. Even the nights are beautiful with the stars overhead so abundant that one can go years without seeing such a sight in the east. The next day we left our tents behind and hiked to Lonesome Lake at the base of the Cirque of the Towers, a half arc of sharp barren peaks some four-thousand feet above you. Such sights are alien to the southeastern hiker, and they are the reason that we came. There were snowfields on the trail to cross, even though it was July.

When we finished the hike late in the day, we decided to go to the nearest small town and spend the night. There weren't many accommodations in the town, and we stayed in a motel with a strange resemblance to the Bates Motel of movie fame. We probably could have camped in more comfort on the trail. In the course of the events the commode overflowed, which turned out to be an opportunity to talk to the motel owner when he came for repairs. He was from San Francisco, but he said, "I came out here and saw this place, went back home, sold everything I had and moved here." I have never been to San Francisco, but it is reputed to be a beautiful city, so the owner was obviously a person who liked remote places with few people.

We inquired of him concerning a certain hiking trail that was of interest to us and he said we would need to get authorization to hike there as this area is not part of the national forest. "It is just like a ranch, and people will be upset if you travel on it without permission." Recalling the barren moonscape of scrub brush that leads up to the mountains, it was hard to imagine anyone upset with our crossing that desolation, but I am an Easterner insensitive to Western values.

We mentioned that we had left our tent and gear behind while we day-hiked in the area and asked if that was ever a problem. He related an incident where a lone hiker had done that and returned to his campsite and found many items stolen. In looking around he discovered they were taken by two hikers nearby and one was slumbering in his purloined sleeping bag. Our offended hiker took out his hunting knife, grabbed the snoozing thief by his beard, put the knife to the offender's throat and told the thief's partner to gather and return all his stolen items. The man in the sleeping bag, with the knife to his throat, gave considerable vocal encouragement to his partner to expeditiously gather everything together and return all the gear to their new acquaintance. The motel owner said the hiker reported the incident to the police when he came out, and the local police said he had handled the problem exactly right. With a dryness in my own mouth, I reflected that western frontier justice is still alive in Wyoming.

We went to the Grand Teton National Park where we had planned to make a large loop hike of some four days and once again had to obtain permits to camp in the pristine wilderness. Here you are just given a general area in which to camp, not a specific and prepared site as in the Smokies. We parked our car at Jenny Lake and started out with some reservations, as the weather was bad and the forecast was for it to be that way for several days. But when your airline tickets say a certain date and your family and employer expect to see you back at a fixed time, you persevere. The first leg of our trip was to be the least interesting scenic-wise, meandering though nondescript forest, for if you have seen one lodgepole pine, you have seen them all. We set up our tents in the rain and spent the night in increasing discomfort in an area with the ominous name of Death Canyon. Hiking is supposed to be fun, but on occasion it can be more of an ordeal than one encounters in the normal sedate life. The next morning, with more rain and no prospect on an opportunity to see the sights we had come to behold, we decided to cancel this part of the trip and regroup in the comfort of a motel in Jackson Hole. The only problem was that we were ten miles from our car if we backtracked on the trail, and only two miles from a road that was then fifteen miles from our car. We hiked to the road, and I offered to hitchhike to our car, or at worst, to walk it, while Robert stayed with our paraphernalia. Now, I had never hitchhiked in my life.

One of my reasons for hiking and backpacking is to overcome my very strong tendency to get in a comfortable rut and never leave it. And so I seek adventure on the trail, but hitchhiking didn't figure into this equation. I went down to the main road thinking that I was not likely to get a ride because my disheveled hiking clothes, which are never a fashion statement, were wet and muddy and I had a beard that further enhanced my derelict appearance. I put out my thumb and two cars roared by when, to my amazement, a nattily-dressed bearded man in a little sports car stopped and offered me a ride. I found out that my benefactor was a piano player from San Francisco who had just arrived to work in the lounge at a local hotel. He detoured out of his way to drop me off at our car. Piano players from San Francisco will forever hold a special place in my heart for that help in my time of need.

The next day we started again our attempt to penetrate the backcountry of the Tetons, but did take a boat ride across Lake Jenny to start up the Cascade Canyon trail. I was particularly glad to be on this section again, as the pictures of it when my wife and I had been here previously had been ruined in development. The beauty of it all struck me again with a sense of being in the perfect western landscape. This narrow cut of land was created by glaciers so long ago that it was a place lost to the normal pace of life in the "real world." As we walked along, we encountered hikers coming the other way who whispered, "There is a moose up ahead." We scanned each side of this constricted canyon hoping to get a glance of this magnificent but shy creature. When we rounded a corner, we saw the moose sauntering down the center of the trail like any other hiker. We stepped a few feet off the trail and took pictures as it went past, the moose never breaking its own stride and only flinching slightly to the sounds of the clicking of cameras. I guess hikers are part of its natural habitat from the moose's point of view, and like so many animals in national parks it possessed a knowledge that man is not a threat to it in this location.

That night we pitched camp at the base of several mountains, with Grand Teton and Mount Owen rising majestically above us. Part of the wonder of hiking is that magic moments can come so unexpectedly. We were sitting in our campsite finishing dinner when I glanced up to see the top of the peaks in a fiery radiance. I had seen alpine glow in paintings, but I didn't realize the dramatic impact of such a sight. I grabbed my camera to capture the fleeing moment, and in a few minutes it was gone. However, for such things, the radiance continues within and lives on for years as a highlight of our own brief existence here.

The next day was less magical as we ascended to the appropriately named Alaska Basin, which is the opposite side of the three Tetons. Millions of unadventurous tourists don't get to see this side, but neither did we because of the rainy weather. Many places can be awe-inspiring and soul-enriching in the bright sunshine, but the Alaska Basin was depressing in the fog and the mist. It is a barren rocky landscape with scrawny plants and an occasional tree to hang up your food supply from marauding bears. We went to sleep that night listening to the rain pelt against the tent. The next morning all was very quiet, and I was elated to realize that the rain had stopped but deflated when I looked out and saw it snowing. Now, this was in July and we had left behind a heat wave in Knoxville, with temperatures over a hundred. Now we dwelled in a snow-covered countryside. Fortunately, we were warm in our down jackets. We had come prepared, based on the book knowledge of the likely extremes in the West— from being fried by day and frozen at night. Someday I might yet have the view from Alaska Basin but not on this trip, as we returned to our familiar rented car with the Wisconsin plates.

Happily for all vacationers, Yellowstone is right next to Grand Teton, and we went up there to check out the myriad wonders. We were considering hiking into the back country, away from the double circle of the main road in the park, to be away from the madding crowds. However, fear makes cowards of us all. When we went to the ranger station and saw several camping sites closed because of problems with grizzly bears, the urge for adventure departed from our souls. We camped that night on a small plot of ground rented from the park service at the Bridge Bay campground. Although we were surrounded by hundreds of people in their tents, campers and RVs, I still slept a restless slumber knowing that grizzlies could be nearby, no Jeremiah Johnson am I. The memory of reading of the gruesome death of several backpackers by grizzles in Glacier National Park was still too fresh in my mind.

Thus, our experience with Yellowstone consisted of short day hikes and the time-honored tourist route of driving to an attraction and walking across the parking lot to see it. Yellowstone must surely be the most unique place on earth for geological formations. One can only be thankful for the exploration party in 1870 that around a campfire one long-ago night developed the idea of the first national park in the world. The hike along the trail of boardwalks in the Upper Geyser Basin borders on trepidation, as the earth is active all around you. In normal hiking, one fears rock slides, but here the earth bubbles and gurgles and unexpectedly erupts superheated water in geysers at you. As with so much of nature, it must be experienced in person to truly grasp the overwhelming forces that lie deep beneath our feet but exist near the surface in Yellowstone. The crystallized terraces and boiling ponds of the Mammoth Hot Springs appear as if from the torrid surface of Io rather than our own placid Earth. The waterfalls of Yellowstone Falls and Tower Falls look like a set for a Star Wars movie rather than a random creation of nature. One ponders the reaction of the first Indians who traversed this area on their continuing migration from the Bering Strait. Surely this is a place where the gods are angry but paint death in brilliant colors.

The opposite of the heights of the high peaks are inverted mountains called canyons and my wife and I had the opportunity to visit the greatest of all, the Grand Canyon. Standing at the Watchtower overlook at the east end and scanning down the length of the chasm must surely be the greatest visual experience on earth.

There was not time for a lengthy hike but I did take a three-mile trip by myself down its most famous trail, Bright Angel Trail. Usually I would not hike alone, but so many people are on that trail that someone would be by shortly if I needed assistance, plus it is the only trail I know that has emergency phones along the way in case there is an extreme problem. I started at sunrise on a June day and enjoyed the continuous views and the changing light on the rocks. Far below, one can see the faint string of the trail as it winds its way to the thin thread of the river above. With reluctance, I turned around near the first rest house, but with the increasing heat of the day, even in the morning hours, there was indication of what the day would be like. Some hardy souls can make the trip of sixteen miles to the Phantom Ranch at the river and back in one day, but most plan an overnight stay or even a three- to four-day hike for the trip. The Grand Canyon has some truly unique challenges for any American hiker. The elevation difference in the trail is an amazing five-thousand feet which is far more than most trails. It has the additional difficulty of being the reverse of normal hiking in first walking downhill and then having to ascend. Therefore, a one-day trip is particularly difficult because one is facing the steep uphill pitch when already tired. Also, unlike many western mountain trails where water is plentiful, there are only a few places where water is available on the trail. Also, with temperatures being much hotter in the canyon than in surrounding areas, reaching 120 in the summer, one must be very conscious of the liquid supply. All these sobering facts are reinforced by the many park signs that say it will cost you big bucks if the park service has to come and rescue you. Nevertheless, because so many tourists come to the area, this often involves the worst of all challengers to the wilderness— the unprepared and the under-conditioned. The pain of hiking reaches out quickly to such imprudent souls and frequently causes inconvenience or even danger to those who must save them from their folly.

The western lands are so different from the east as to make one wonder how it can all be part of the same country. Even the human culture can be very different, as we discovered in New Mexico with its amazing mixture of Indian, Hispanic and Anglo cultures, all intermingled in a fascinating montage. The terrain itself is more varied, as you can drive from deep forest to high mountains to waterless desert to impassible canyons in a brief time. To hike this diverse landscape and to know its richness would take several lifetimes, so being a mere mortal I can only briefly sample its richness.

Trails of Wrathful Waters

Despite my chosen hobby of walking in the woods, there are other ways to experience the wilderness than by hiking on a trail. In the interest of giving other outdoor pursuits a fair assessment, and, more importantly, to accommodate a brother-in-law, I entrusted my fate to whitewater rafting. This is not a sport I would choose of my own accord, but being married, one acquires companions with whom association would be unlikely otherwise. Gary is a congenial type but bears a close resemblance to Fidel Castro and has an affinity for Harley-Davidson motorcycles that I am somehow lacking. We must have appeared to be a bizarre couple traversing around, because I am your basic Bob Newhart kind of guy. Fortunately, Gary and I shared enthusiasm for outdoor pursuits, although his was more water-related than land-based. Despite my being raised in Florida, with the ocean on three sides and having worked for an organization dedicated to creating lakes in the Tennessee Valley, I have never really cared for water recreation.

However, Gary, being from Missouri, certainly welcomed the opportunity to sample the joys of mountain rivers so lacking in his native environment. As one always interested in new experiences, I was more than willing to give it a try. In southeast Tennessee, there is a stretch of the Ocoee River so perfect for whitewater activities that it was used for the kayaking events in the 1996 Olympics. The Ocoee is one of the rivers managed under the TVA system, but for many years its potential for whitewater rafting was not apparent because the river seldom flowed freely. The power company prior to the existence of TVA had built a flume of five miles to carry the water from upstream to a downstream power house, leaving only a long segment of bare rocky riverbed. When TVA closed the flume for significant repairs, the water roared joyfully and merrily down the rocky gully. At this point, kayaking enthusiasts discovered one of the best whitewater stretches in Eastern United States. When the flume repairs were finished seven years later, and after some prickly negotiations between TVA and concerned recreation interests, agreement was reached to share the water with these activities.

In order to partake of this wonder, we availed ourselves of commercial outfitters. Gary had experience at this sort of thing, but as a total novice, I was very attentive to the instructions on proper technique. As the fifth person in our raft was a trained guide, the likelihood of our getting into serious trouble seemingly was at a minimum. The four-hour trip was one of sheer joy as we descended through rapids that rocked us roughly and gave an edge of danger to the prospect of being flipped into this unforgiving maelstrom. To inspire awe and some fear, the major rapids had such colorful names as Grumpy, Double Trouble and Table-saw.

This was a new way for me to savor nature and its forces, ignoring the fact that our raft was guided by a seasoned oarsman and that a road paralleled the river. We accepted the challenge of being battered jerkily about in the rapids with the ever-present prospect of sudden submersion in angry torrents if our steward guide or inexperienced crew made a costly blunder. Between the episodes of high water and intense paddling, we enjoyed stretches of tranquility where the flow was gentle and we could enjoy the beauty of the green canyon that drifted gently past with little effort on our part. While trudging along the trail there is rarely any real and imminent danger comparable to what one faces as swirling rapids loom and one wonders if a flimsy craft and all its occupants will be present at the other end.

The intensity and focus required on a continuous basis on the effort at hand is worlds away from a stroll in the woods where one's mind can wander far from the serene setting. Of course, I seldom do any rock-scrambling and never any mountain climbing with technical gear that would necessitate a similar concentration. White water is thrilling but, for me, to be experienced only briefly, as my goal in the wilderness is to seek tranquility.

Nevertheless, I did take my two teenage daughters on this trip down the Ocoee and they watched in despair as their father was thrown overboard at the first turbulence we encountered. A delusion of appearing heroic before one's offspring sometimes meets a harsh reality. But the memories were many from this trip, including a lingering time at a swimming pond where they could enjoy the rare peace of gentle water in this angry river.

Gary, being a generous soul, arranged for me to enjoy the delights of the Missouri River on one of our many family visits to the Show Me State. He had a large canoe and gathered together all the necessary equipment and supplies for a river journey on the Mighty Mo. We put in near the bridge of the I-40 interstate over the Missouri and planned to go the thirty-five miles downstream to the state capital, Jefferson City. The Missouri River at this point is free flowing, but progresses indolently under normal conditions, so to make any significant progress we had to put our backs into the rowing. As we gently glided down river, there were ample opportunities to leisurely watch the occasional bird and enjoy the serenity of the tree-lined banks. Having traveled on the Tennessee River on several occasions, I expected to see homes and other manmade structures on the river banks, but the Tennessee River is essentially a series of lakes, with the water levels carefully controlled by my friends in Reservoir Operations. On the other hand, only limited flood control exists on this stretch of the Missouri River and few individuals would build on the flood plain. Consequently, there are mile after mile of forested shores with only sparse evidence of human settlement—an echo of the time Louis and Clark traveled the area.

I must confess that I find most river travel rather boring. When something of interest is seen, it is at a tantalizing distance that remains unexplored. Once an unusual feature is encountered on the trail, unless it is a distant view, it can be thoroughly explored or in some cases battled with. However this languorous river was not without its periodic excitement in the form of tugs pushing large barges. What made this gripping for us was the wakes created in their passage, as we had to be alert to steer the canoe directly at them and ride over their crest or our fragile craft would be swamped.

This was a two-day trip and Gary knew of a small island in the river where we could camp. Calling it an island is probably generous, as it was little more than a sandbar without a tree or significant vegetation. But as no floods were expected, it served us as an ideal stop for the night, untroubled by fellow humans. There was sufficient driftwood on the island to make a very satisfactory bonfire in the evening. We slept peacefully at night, only hearing an occasional tug with its barges going by and hoping its sonar was adequate to avoid the diminutive shoal that was our temporary home. The whole trip was an excellent way to view a section of Missouri that I had not realized was so well preserved and to visualize Mark Twain's life on the river.

With the adventure of the Ocoee and the serenity of the Missouri behind us, we were ready for even greater challenges of the wild waters of the wilderness. In the course of researching for the next Missouri family visit to Tennessee I found tourist brochures touting the glories of the Nolichucky River in upper Tennessee. This is a river without dams on its upper reaches, so it is unpredictable whether the river will be a satisfying torrent or a tiresome series of ponds to drag a craft across. The commercial outfitter had the usually large rafts with a guide, but also provided small one-person rafts that they called funyaks. The brochure stated that you had to be twelve years old to handle a funyak, and I decided that if a twelve-year-old could handle it, a funyak shouldn't be too difficult for me and effortless for Gary. Little did I know then that twelve-year-olds in Uncoi County are made of stern stuff. They must be a far cut above your average couch potato, video-playing adolescent. The very kindly outfitters also provided a campsite at their base, and Gary and I innocently spent a night next to the gently babbling liquid dragon we would dare to confront the next day.

The next morning dawned with overcast skies and intermittent light rain. This was disappointing, but as we were going to be on the river, getting wet by rain didn't seem to matter greatly. The outfitters hauled our gallant party of fun-seekers ten miles up the river. We had large rafts for most of the group, but eight of us were in our individual funyak. Our flotilla of funyaks included an experienced guide to instruct us in the proper techniques. At the initial rapid, we were told that the funyaks would go first, followed by the big rafts to pick up any of us that didn't make it through the rapids in our small craft, which didn't strike me as very comforting at this stage of the event. Our guide said, "OK, on this rapid keep as close to the left bank as you can and when you get to the bottom row for all you're worth to the right side." As the second funyak, I entered the rapid and almost immediately knew I had little control over my fate. The turbulent water rushing down between the many boulders bounced me to and fro, but I did manage to keep the little raft pointed in the right direction as I flayed away with my two-ended paddle. When I hit the whirlpool at the bottom of the rapid I attempted to faithfully execute my instructor's direction and did succeed in rowing to the right bank to join the other funyak. Regaining some composure and feeling pride that I had come through that wall of water solely on my own efforts, I awaited the others.

Eventually all the funyaks appeared except for the one piloted by Gary. After an anxious wait, I was alarmed to see Gary's funyak float by upside down and no Gary in sight. One of the more difficult prospects in life is to explain to a sister-in-law what happened to her husband on an outing, particularly as this was the sister who elected to stay behind on the Alum Cave Bluff hike. With relief I saw one of the larger rafts come by with Gary sitting sheepishly in the bow like some Captain Ahab who didn't get the whale. This first rapid was where the outfitter had set up a camera to take a series of three pictures to sell to us after the trip. In Gary's case, the first picture showed him braving the rapid, the second was of him turning over and the third showed only a tennis shoe sticking out of the frothy turbulence.

There were some six major rapids on this trip, and on each Gary and I were determined to make it through without hitting the drink again. This beautiful canyon could be only enjoyed for short spells until our guide would gather us together again like a mother hen with her chicks and explain patiently what was expected of us to survive the next rapid. With each rapid I gathered more confidence, along with a growing resolve to never again submit myself to such a situation where my control was very marginal. I am sure a veteran of whitewater sports would enjoy all this greatly, but my pleasure was far outweighed by the pain of the unknown, coupled with the uncertainly that I could perform adequately at the next rapid.

Finally, we came to the last rapid only a short distance from the base camp. I had made the entire trip without being thrown from my mis-named funyak. The last rapid appeared only as a two-foot drop-off, mild compared to what we had been through. However, unknown to me, its tricky swirls gave funyaks more problems than the previous ones, and camp personnel would gather on the shore to watch the show of paying customers upended and separated from their small rafts. As I approached the rapid, I lost control and went into the rapid sideways. Everything seemed to happen in slow motion and I was powerless to control it. As the funyak dropped on its side, it rapidly filled with water and soon flipped over, throwing me into the churning waters. Under I went, even with a life jacket on. As I came to the surface I discovered that the funyak was on top of me, and since no amount of thrashing could get it off of me and I stayed under water. As my breath started to run out, the thought crossed my mind that this is what it is like to drown and that I was going to die there in that river. Finally I was able to push the funyak away and popped to the surface for air, coughing and gagging. As I struggled to gasp in the sweet air, I heard above the roar of the river laughter from the camp personnel who were enjoying my travails. I am not by nature a violent person, but if I could have gotten one of them by their mirthful throat at that instance I would have joyfully squeezed hard.

Gary and I did survive the trip and with its many dangerous experiences. The later retelling of the adventures in calmer settings made it worthwhile and provided a lasting satisfaction for having accomplished it. However, the punishing river was not yet finished with me. We had started the day in rain, but it cleared at noon and the sun gave welcome warmth to our trip. When one hikes in the East in the summer sunburn is not a concern, but we had spent several hours in the river without shade and in swimming trunks. Shortly after the trip, I developed a fierce sunburn that provided a lingering pain and severely limited my capacity as a host for the family visit.

These misadventures convinced me that I wanted to experience the wilderness from the trails on solid earth rather than know the highs of conquering white water. A friend did try kayaking and I would discuss it with him to gain a further sense of this sport. He trained at the swimming pool at the local YMCA, where he would practice flipping over his kayak and righting it again, as all skilled kayakers can do. One day I saw him with a nasty cut on his forehead and I asked him what happened. "Well Dave, I was kayaking on the Obed when I turned over in the rapids. I tried to right myself but the force of flowing waters are greatly different than the calmness of the pool at the Y. I couldn't right myself and unbuckled from the kayak to swim to the surface. However in this frothy world, I had no sense of direction and swam instead to the bottom and hit my head on a rock." Later he told me he gave up the sport because he could practice it only once a month and to become good enough to enjoy it with the necessary skills he would have to do it at least once a week. This left me grateful for hiking as the skills are so low that as one can do it after months or years without facing life threatening situations because of a lack of practice. However, the memory of turbulent water pulling at me in a wild river provided another reminiscence of life away from civilized life.

Hiking the Urban Environment

The lessons of hiking can be applied in all situations; everything I need to know about life, I learned on the trail. If you master the rules of hiking in the wilds, then you can confidently apply them anywhere and feel secure to face whatever comes your way in the wilderness of life. Likewise the resourceful hiker always finds suitable hiking areas no matter where he or she dwells.

It has been my fate in life to sometimes find myself in extraordinary state of affairs that I had never envisioned. Being basically a small-town person and loving the open country nearby, the thought of living in a large city never entered my calculations. Furthermore, even with a fertile imagination, I had never once conceived of myself as serving as a foreign missionary. However, being married, one's spouse does conjure up many opportunities and directions not anticipated as a single individual. Thus it came to pass that our interest in the mission field and a persistent inner voice lead us to apply to the International Mission Board of the Southern Baptist Convention for consideration of assignment in a land far from our comfort zone. We were past the age and inclination to be career missionaries, but the Mission Board offers many short-term assignments of a few years duration.

The usual image of a missionary is one who works with the poorest of people in third-world countries. I could see myself in some downtrodden but exotic part of the world with wonderful hiking opportunities in our free time. Most missionaries are in developing countries, but many things in my life never fit conventional patterns. Thus, through an unusual chain of events, we were assigned not to some remote village on the edge of an untamed wilderness but to the greatest city in the world, Paris, France. We were delighted at the prospect of living in the city on the Seine, if a bit overwhelmed. Additionally, our "target group" was not the poor people of Paris, but the executive population, based on the assumption that if you can reach those at the top, that will have an impact all the way down. Not your normal group to witness to by any means, but when you read the Bible carefully you find that Jesus reached out to all levels of society. That included his disciple, Matthew, who was a prosperous government contractor, engaged in collecting taxes for a hated occupying power. The last supper was held in "the upper room," and only prosperous people in Jerusalem had two-story homes. Another prominent supporter of Christ was the wealthy Joseph of Arimathaea, in whose tomb Jesus was buried. With that prospect, we closed down the house, said goodbye to kin, our cat and a coterie of friends, and embarked on strange paths.

Now, going from our home in Knoxville, Tennessee, to the City of Light represented a cultural challenge of the first magnitude, particularly for a person who prefers life on the trail in secluded locations. But I had every confidence that even though in a very unfamiliar environment I could find opportunities to pursue my hobby. Actually, if you view Paris as just another large wilderness and its boulevards as well constructed hiking trails, there are few problems that can't be handled if you employ the lessons learned in other hinterlands.

As in all hiking, the first consideration is what to wear and what equipment to carry, all focused on functionality and light weight. Naturally, the first item to consider is proper footwear if extended walking under varying conditions is involved. Normally, I would wear tennis shoes on sidewalks or level terrain, but one thing a foreigner doesn't want to do is look like a tourist. No Frenchman my age would wear tennis shoes unless he was going to actually play tennis, or more likely, a casual game of football (soccer). Generally, dress shoes aren't suitable for extensive walking, and because it rains almost every day in the north of France they would be impracticable. I selected a brown Earth shoe with soles like a hiking boot that proved to be ideal in all situations I encountered on the trails of Paris.

As for appropriate attire, the people of Paris dress surprisingly causally. One never sees any person wearing those crazy outfits one sees in fashion shows on television. At least we never did, but then maybe missionaries aren't invited to the best parties where someone would actually wear an outrageous outfit that looks like it was designed by a circus clown for satire and then call it haute couture. Except for business and professional people, the average Parisian dresses in very serviceable clothing to saunter a large city on foot and by subway. Consequently, the clothes that I had brought were sufficient, except for the shirt that said "This Is Big Orange Country."

In the normal course of hiking in Paris, one must always carry several items. As in all explorations, good maps are essential. Except for the boulevards, much of Paris is a confusing maze of streets, even in newer sections. In much of Europe, the concept of a four-corner city block and a metropolis based on a grid system is held in distain, so it is easy for any courageous hiker to become very confused, with the possibility of hiking in circles—always an inner fear of all hikers. Furthermore, French streets have a tendency to change names every five blocks or so. My personal guess is that there are so many famous people for whom they wish to name streets, that each famous person can't have a section of street or boulevard of more than a few blocks. The Parisians have generously named several streets after Americans, such as Rue Ernest Hemingway, Avenue du Président Kennedy, Place du Général Patton and Boulevard Pershing. But even these illustrious Americans may still have to share their street with another famous individual. In Nanterre, where we lived, part of a major street is named after Woodrow Wilson, then for a former French prime minister, and finally the same street is named after V. I. Lenin. I have often wondered what Woody would have thought about sharing his street with Lenin. We lived on Rue Salvador Allende, which seemed like a strange address for American missionaries, considering he was a Marxist president of Chile who committed suicide during an alleged CIA coup to overthrow him. Good maps are vital to keep it all straight or you will become more lost than if following cow paths on the open range.

Additionally, good maps are a necessity to keep track of the very excellent transportation system in Paris. The Metro and RER trains and subways will place you usually within a few blocks of where you want to be and, if not, there is always the bus system. The only downside is that one of the favorite pastimes of working Parisians is the *grève*, or strike, with a one-day strike being particularly popular. Local residents listen to the radio each morning to find out where a strike is occurring and make plans accordingly, rather like getting the report on weather or traffic jams. As I did not know French that well, I was often caught unawares, but this merely afforded extra opportunities for hiking. One never knows what unexpected obstacle will be encountered on the trail.

Other items are important to carry, such as an umbrella, for even if the sky is clear in the morning there will likely be rain some time during the day. It is always nice to carry a camera to record sights on the trail, but it needs to be hidden away or you will be identified as *un touriste* which is the last thing you want to happen. There can be quite a lot of gear for hiking the byways of Paris, creating the need for a briefcase of some kind, which is very normal accessory for French men. Part of the reason for this is that a French driver's license is so large that it won't fit into a wallet. I routinely carried a large bag with a shoulder strap for all my paraphernalia and blended right in.

Always in hiking, one of the most interesting dimensions is the people you encounter. All my life I have heard that the French are rude to Americans. However, after living there for several months, the true situation came into perspective. Actually the French are among the most polite people on earth. The subways can be very crowded, but when you arrive at a stop, the mob preparing to board will wait until everyone gets off before attempting to climb aboard. If you are packed in the middle of a multitude in the train when it is time for your stop, just start saying "Pardon, pardon" and the horde will part like you are Moses at the Red Sea. So if the French are so polite, why are they rude to Americans? The problem comes when American behave in ways that the French consider barbaric. The French are a very quiet people, and except for some rambunctious youth you will not hear loud talking, even on the subway platforms and never in a restaurant. If you hear a loud group at a restaurant or on the street it is usually Americans. Also, waiters and waitresses expect to be treated very politely, and if you don't have the proper deference life at the restaurant can be even more lengthy than is normal and normal can be quite long. The concept that "the customer is always right" is alien to the French mind, particularly to the waiters on the Champs-Élysées. As one who has lived in the American South, with its reputation for courtesy, I had to notch up my politeness several levels, and when I did not I paid the price. But as in all hiking, when you know what is expected of you on the trail things do run much smoother. Except for a few grouches and drunks that you find in any culture, the French really do like Americans who follow their standards while in their country.

It is always important to assess the risks involved in life on the trail. Given that you are in a city, stream crossings, landslides, and constant exposure to inclement weather don't pose the usual challenges. However there are many animals and people about. The French love dogs and you will encounter a lot of them, but not to worry, because the French have trained them to be highly disciplined. Almost all dogs will be on a leash, and as they are constantly in crowds, they do not seem to be bothered as you approach or stay close. I guess if you stepped on one in the subway it might make an issue of the matter, but their main expectations are to be petted by all, even strangers. Given the number of dogs, it is amazing how seldom you hear one bark; apparently they have been taught not to do that. The only issue for Americans is that dogs are allowed in restaurants. The first time I saw a dog sitting in the chair next to me I kept a close eye on him in case he went for my hamburger.

As mentioned earlier, the French are very polite, except for those who want to rob you (a sizable population in itself) and who tend to be much less considerate than others. It is not likely that someone will pull a gun on you, but the more subtle practice of pick pocketing is so wide spread and skillfully practiced that there must be schools for it. I have never been physically robbed in the United States, but in the year and a half I was in France I twice had to fight off pickpockets in the subway, and once could not prevent thieves from snatching my wife's purse. Paris may be the City of Love, but I never detected any desire for my body; however, there was considerable lust for my wallet. Doing church work, one tends to dress up on occasion, and each of these incidents occurred while we were in our Sunday best and others heard us speaking English. In populated areas as well as on the trail, it is important to blend in with the native population.

As in all hiking, the fundamental requirements of life become important, and I am forced to focus on food more than I usually do. I am no connoisseur of fine cuisine, and like my cat, could probably eat the same thing every day without thinking too much about it. I eat because it is necessary to sustain life, but if there was an alternative I would not miss my repasts without regrets. It is tragic that a person of such plebian tastes would live in a place where food is considered second only to sex in its importance to life. An American must be careful what he orders to avoid some very unpleasant surprises. Despite stupendous efforts, my French language skills remained at a very rudimentary level and consequentially I ate a lot more meals of ham than I would have preferred because of the simple fact that I knew *jambon* meant *pig*. Later on in my French lessons I learned that *cheval* means *horse*, and the French have no qualms about eating Trigger. I guess eating a horse is not significantly different from eating a cow or a deer, but I could never overcome my cultural limitations. While I am your basic meat-and-potatoes person, my wife is always fond of trying something different. This led to several unfortunate instances when she could not bring herself to eat what she had ordered in her adventure in fine dining. I had to order with the thought that I might be sharing my meal with her, or worse, switching our meals and eating something that I had not the faintest idea of what it was. My wife likes beef well-cooked, while the French relish meat that is almost raw. Despite repeating *"bien cuit"* emphatically, the meat would frequently come out blood red, and even after a return trip to the kitchen a typical chef would not alter his standards. Consequently, we would often trade dinners and I would eat something that I was afraid was not dead enough to peacefully accept my eating it. Eating on the trail in Paris was a greater challenge than on any wilderness path.

In Paris I did much of the food shopping. Due to my limited French, that meant I could never ask a question if I was having trouble finding an item. Consequently, after hiking up and down many an aisle at French grocery stores, I have a very clear picture of their typical inventory. A favorite food of mine is peanut butter, which is a foreign food for the French and is only to be found in the ethnic food section, which reinforced my feeling of being an outsider. Some provisions favored by hikers are not to be found in all of France, such as Oreo cookies and Fig Newtons. While a moderate fan of them in the U.S., in France they became a rare delicacy for expatriate Americans. When people came from the states to visit missionaries and inquired ahead about what to bring, the inevitable request was for Oleo cookies, and thus the proud missionary could be ensured of a successful gathering of Americans if he were able to serve up such a delight.

The resourceful hiker always tries to adapt to the environment in which he temporarily inhabits, which brings us to the matter of culture. Some people are under the false impression that a hidden agenda of all missionaries is to share the civilized ways of the homeland with the simple natives one is working with. I am skeptical of the truth of this assertion, but I was prepared to bring the superior culture of East Tennessee to the indigenous population of Île-de-France. The French claim to be refined, but never once did I see an advertisement for a tractor pull or a WFA wresting match the whole time I was in Paris. If you tell a French person you are from Tennessee, the reaction is inevitably the same; they respond excitedly with "Jack Daniels," which is not the image one wants to project as a Southern Baptist missionary. Indeed, one of the fourteen fireable offences as a missionary is to drink any alcoholic beverage, including wine. Try to explain that to the French, even to those who are strongly religiously committed.

While hiking around Paris, there are numerous worthwhile sights and many bewildering ones. In many ways, the terrain is amazingly uniform. There are tall cathedrals and monuments, but French have kept Paris beautiful by not allowing any building over six stories high in Paris itself. This leaves a very spacious feel to the place that would be destroyed if you were walking down canyons of skyscrapers. The highly impressive Arc de Triomphe would seem mundane if it were surrounded by fifty-story glass monsters. A person on foot is offered an excellent opportunity to observe the beautiful and varied architecture, which is an amazing mix of every style imaginable. The French do not hesitate to place an ultra-modern avant-garde building next to a seventeenth-century palace, as the controversial glass pyramids in the courtyard of the Louvre will testify.

One building that fascinated me is the Pompidou Center, the modern art gallery with all the normally hidden utilities of elevators, ductwork and support beams on the outside, which has a surprisingly pleasing effect.

However, in walking around the exhibits on the inside, one is left in a permanent state of bewilderment. One exhibit is a smashed up piano which represented the artist's protest against something or other. There is a painting that is simply solid blue, which has inspired me to attempt a solid purple painting someday that will surely be worth a fortune. The magnificence of the building stands in stark contrast to its contents, which appears to be a trend among modern art museums. Some friends visited the highly innovative new Guggenheim Museum in Bilbao, Spain, and said they loved the building but were disappointed in the exhibits, one being simply tiles on the floor, which was the artist's protest against "verticality in art." All this leads me to the conclusion that a modern art museum is a hundred-million-dollar building with six-hundred dollars worth of art in it.

It is the natural instinct of all hikers to seek the high places on the trail for the inspiring vistas they offer, and such a tendency can be satisfied even in a man-made setting. The obvious choice in Paris is the Eiffel Tower with its glorious views of Paris from the top. As a hiker, one prefers to obtain the heights through strenuous physical efforts, a feat not possible with the Eiffel Tower other than at the first level. Other limited opportunities are available, however, for some uphill work. The Arc de Triomphe is 164 feet high, and as the elevator runs on an uncertain schedule and is generally reserved for the handicapped, one obtains this summit by a long climb up a circular stairway. Views from the top are always better if one is a bit breathless. The physical highpoint in Paris is the Montmarte area, a locale popular with local artists and with wonderful views of Paris. Here again there are climbing opportunities, for on the summit is the modern cathedral of Sacré-Cœur which has a well placed bell tower of 252 feet that one can ascend to near the top. While I am not a huge fan of cityscapes, Paris is inspiring when viewed from any direction, even for nature lovers.

David Curran

Another of the great charms of Paris is its numerous parks, with an amazing amount of well-cultured vegetation for the hiker to enjoy. We were assigned to attend a language school on the Left Bank for several months, and those four hours of class each day were total misery for me and my flat learning curve for other tongues. Near to our college was Luxembourg Gardens, and the thought of our daily stroll through it was one of the few positive thoughts I could muster in this daily humiliation of my shortcomings. The horticulture budget of the city of Paris must exceed most other line items for all was exceedingly well tended and varied over time. The greenery of the city lent a frequent feeling of the countryside even with the sound of traffic nearby. In Nantere, we lived in a gigantic apartment complex, but a spacious city park was next to us, which I would walk through frequently, at least during the day, for the night held too many forest ogres that preyed on the unwary. The park had a pleasant pond of a marshy sort with wild ducks, so that by focusing your attention, you could be transported to a serene glen miles from city life.

We did not travel much from Paris, but a favorite place was Monet's house and gardens. Part of the gardens are a virtual jungle of flowers, trees, and undergrowth, all lovingly restored to near the condition that he used for inspiration for revolutionizing the very nature of painting to the impressionistic style. We went there both in the spring and the fall to experience the changing setting and to escape into his world of colorful forms. Indeed, a short distance from Paris in any direction took one into a surprisingly sparse countryside, as the medieval European practice dictated that people would live in villages for protection rather than the American habit of isolated farm houses. On returning to Paris one Sunday evening we were shocked to be sitting in traffic jams similar to any rush hour. Upon inquiry, we learned that the Parisians also love the countryside and would have a home in a rural community for the week-end or return to the ancestral abode for a time away from city life. The joy of natural surroundings resides deep, even in lands heavily populated for thousands of years.

For work and for pleasure, I walked many miles of Paris streets and boulevards and experienced the full range of emotions that one feels in the inaccessible wilderness. There is the thrill of new discoveries, of vistas unexpected, of an unbelievable variety of people and, yes, risks and pain if proper precautions are not observed. So, be brave oh wondrous hiker, for even in the urban wilderness, one can create opportunities to practice your skill and survive and thrive in even the most unlikely of settings for our noble calling.

Sweat and Fears on New England Trails

The search for new horizons is continual for the restless hiker, with the constant desire to know what is over the next ridge. After extensively hiking the Appalachian Trail in the south, Robert and I became curious to savor what it is like at the northern end. We had been told that the middle can be somewhat boring, without the ruggedness and spectacular beauty of the Smokies, but that the New England section, with peaks nearly as high as the Smokies, has its own daunting wonders. Duly we planned a trip to the highest northern part of the AT, Mt. Washington in New Hampshire.

In doing the research, I excitedly assured Robert that we would have a different hiking experience from our southern jaunts. As we drove through Vermont and New Hampshire, the mountains looked amazingly like those back home. Robert said somewhat skeptically, "You mean we drove fifteen-hundred miles to hike in East Tennessee?" All I could do was to lamely promise him it would be different, and when the barren tops of the Presidential Range came into view we knew we were in for something unique. How much so was mercifully hidden from us until we walked in its midst. All the AT in the south is below the tree line, but for almost thirteen miles, this range is above where the forest dares to venture. Research and preparation is always important in any endeavor, but sometimes the words on paper don't have the impact of reality on the ground, or in this case on the mountaintop. This is part of the charm and the challenge of hiking in strange places. For some reason, I assumed that the area above the tree line would be like the balds in the Smokies, which are pleasant grass covered meadows. It is amazing how much about life I visualize in my mind that an unforgiving indifferent reality quickly alters. But then part of the joy of hiking is encountering the unexpected and having to cope with it.

We had arranged to stay in the facilities of the Appalachian Mountain Club. The first and last nights of our excursion would be at their base-camp lodge and the middle two nights at their huts along the top of the crest. From a hiker's point of view, this is an organization that truly has its act together. The facilities at Pinkham Notch Camp are ideal for hikers, comfortable but austere, with the addition of a nature lecture that night on the peculiar habits of the beaver to entertain us. The next day we started out with high anticipation and plunged along this fabled section of the AT. The first four miles were pleasant cruising, but at the junction with the Madison Gulf trail the AT starts a 3000-foot ascent to Mt. Madison. Many of the trails in this area are over a hundred years old and were not developed by professional trail planners. Consequently, where in the Smokies there are switchbacks to climb steep sections, here the trail goes straight up the mountain side. We were hiking steadily, when suddenly the trail abruptly ended at the face of a fifteen-foot rock wall. This first encounter was a shock when we realized that the trail resumed at the top of this barrier. It became a frequent occurrence to climb up rock cliffs that fortunately had many small trees and footrests for those on the trail who also happen to be lugging a forty-pound backpack.

It was tough going, and about midway we met a couple near our age resting on the side of the trail. The woman was perky but the man had the demoralized look that only exhaustion can bring. The woman said they were going to the same hut as we were for the night, with the silence of the mountain broken only by the heavy breathing of her husband. We said tentatively that we would see them at the hut, but we never did. There are many unfinished tales of the trail, and we could only assume they exercised personal wisdom and went back down the mountain rather than turn what should be recreation into a potential death march.

As we emerged from the woods into the area above the tree line, the magnitude of what was before us came as a stunning revelation. The thirteen miles above the tree line in New Hampshire turned out not to be pleasant meadows of grass gently swaying in the wind but an endless alpine expanse of boulders. It was all rocks and boulders jumbled so that at every step one had to careful to avoid twisting an ankle or toppling over with the pack onto the jagged surface. On the way up, seemingly by the grace of God, Robert had reached out and accidentally grasped someone's hiking stick that had been left behind. Robert is far stronger than I but not as agile, and as we crossed this sea of rocky rubble for the next three days the stick rescued him many a time from the painful side of hiking.

The views were a fine compensation for the risks incurred, as the weather was fairly clear and we could see the barren grandeur all around us that must be truly unique for eastern America. After much effort we finally topped Mt. Madison and started the descent to our night's lodging. It was apparent why tent camping is prohibited on the top ridge. First, there did not appear to be a suitably level place to pitch a tent on the rocky broken terrain. Secondly, the area is famous for some of the worst weather in the world. The weather station at Mount Washington recorded a wind in 1934 that was the world record for many years at 231 miles per hour. One can only image the fate of tent campers if an unexpected storm appeared. Because of the stony terrain, the trail ahead is often not obvious, so one looks for the rock piles called cairns set up along the way. We were grateful for the clear weather, because trying to find one's way across this in fog, heavy rain, or snowy whiteouts would be more adventure than we sought. Many a story is told in these parts of the sad fate of novices and experienced hikers trapped in unforgiving conditions when the mountain turns savage.

Madison Hut has a solid stoic and reassuring appearance that it would withstand anything the mountain has to offer. Hiking tends to be a solitary adventure, with occasional brief encounters with other hikers. But to stay in a hut is to enter a social milieu that is quite different for ordinary Americans. We are not accustomed to spending a night in such close quarters with others and certainly not in the "wilderness" on the trail. The "hut" can hold fifty people who are crowded into one large room for the night where there are a series of high bunk beds. So you sleep with some forty-eight other strangers of which the main hazard is that someone snoring near you. The hut also has a staff of attractive young Amazons and muscular Greek gods who are usually college students in other seasons. In addition to cooking meals and maintaining the place, they bring in supplies, which involves carrying a ninety-pound pack three-and-a-half miles up the mountain. A strong group they are. We asked them if they had any difficulty hiking on this lunar landscape, particularly with such a heavy load and they assured us that they had adjusted fine. They told the story of how one night they hiked over to the next hut in the darkness, got a piece of furniture as a joke on that hut's crew and carried it back to their hut over the trail Robert and I had difficulty navigating the next day. Some would say their energy level and concept of fun was inspiring and others would attribute it to an outlet for troubled souls overcome with boredom.

In the long evening, one has a chance to chat with fellow adventurers. One young couple was vacationing together. They both had taught at a New England college and had gotten married. Later she had the opportunity to advance her career by heading a college department in Washington State. After some discussion she took the job and he stayed behind. I asked how they grappled with such a situation in their marriage and he said, "We manage to get together on holidays for a very intense time together," which was probably an understatement.

The next day, our hike was very different from our typical experiences in the south, now having constant openness and the changing views. We reached Mt. Adams and could look back to Mt Madison where we had been and came to an appropriately-named area called Thunderstorm Junction. As we hiked, we peered down into the ruggedness of Jefferson Ravine and the Great Gulf Wilderness. They dispelled my stereotype of New England overrun with people. Years later I would visit Scotland and discover some geologists consider the Scottish highlands to be the very northern part of the Appalachian Mountains until the earth's plates separated and the continents drifted apart. Certainly to the untrained eye there is a striking resemblance between what we were seeing here and later saw in Scotland.

Our solitary experience was interrupted again when we came to the people-overrun summit of Mt. Washington. At 6288 feet it is only about 350 feet lower than the highest point on the AT of Clingsmans Dome back in our Smokies. It is possible to drive to the top of Mt. Washington on the east side or use the world's steepest cog railroad from the other. The coal-fired train emitted a profuse black plume that lingered and offended one for this intrusion of civilization, but also charmed as a reminder of a bygone era.

After a brief stay with hordes of people, the inferior ones who had conquered this mountain by car or train, we once again found the quietude of the open trail. We descended down happy in the knowledge that our major uphill experience in New England was finished and we soon passed two high mountain lakes that had a portrait-like quality of reflecting the surrounding white rocks with green and yellow vegetation around them. However, once again we plunged into a mass of humanity when we came to the Lakes of the Clouds Hut named after what we had passed. This hut can hold up to ninety people, which gave even greater opportunity for the snorers among us to serenade others.

The next day we left the AT and went down the Boot Spur trail which came to the Pinkham Notch Camp, where we would complete our circuit. This last trail is remote in that we saw only one other group as we weaved our way down hill and soon left the rocky jumbled moonscape for the forest and once again had the fragrant smell of trees around us. Danger lurks in forms that those from southern climes would never foresee. This trail skirts Tuckerman Ravine. Some ten years after we were there a young woman was killed while skiing in the ravine when large blocks of ice broke off the headwall above and an ice chuck hit her. One of the blocks of ice was estimated to weigh fifteen tons, something unimaginable to those of us from a more temperate zone. And this occurred in the month of June!

In our continuing quest for new hiking experiences, we drove to Acadia National Park on Mount Desert Island in Maine. This is a park different from other national parks, as it is not a continuous land area but a patchwork of private and park lands. The hand of John D. Rockefeller, Jr. is present here, too, as in the Smokies, as he gave some third of the land that makes up the park. When we arrived, the fog was so thick that disappointingly little could be seen. We were told that such fog is frequent and many a visitor has left without appreciating this park. However we decided to stay the night to see if it would clear and spent the evening touring the northern version of our Gatlinburg known as Bar Harbor, with its many upscale and swanky shops that clash so with the seeking of raw and rugged wilderness.

The next day was clear and beautiful and the views we had on our hikes were some of the most impressive ever for us. The combination of red mountains and a cobalt ocean littered with white sailboats was unforgettable. It looked like Hawaii without the palm trees. We hiked the Gorham Mountain Trail which reaches a 525-foot elevation. By normal standards, to hike to the top of such a low knoll would not be worth mentioning, but it arose next to the Frenchman's Bay of the Atlantic

Ocean. To look at the hodgepodge of rocks and ridges around us with such colorful names as the Beehive and to glance in the other direction to see the wine-dark sea, as Homer would say, with a sprinkling of white sailboats drifting in the wind is to encounter one of the finest sights in all my hiking. The magic of the moment of the splendor of rock and sea was to be briefly suspended in that eternal moment where past and present vanish and only a beautiful reality exists.

In addition to the mountains of Acadia it was a pleasure to walk along the rocky coast of beaches of stones and boulders so unlike the soft sands of our southern beaches. To stand and watch the awesome waves beat against the unyielding rocks in this ceaseless battle of land against the sea is to experience again this eternal struggle. Beyond the shore one sees the lobster fishermen attending to their traps to feed the hungry tourists on land. The idyllic scene was somewhat dissipated by the musical preferences of these particular youthful fisherman whose radio blared out loud rock tunes as they went about their monotonous tasks. But Acadia has a uniqueness that sets it apart from other eastern parks despite its small and fragmented domain.

In hiking I always value matchless and different experiences, and in our few days of sampling New England trails we found that the Appalachian Mountains of the north are almost extraterrestrial compared to those of our South. The hike above the tree line and along the ocean bestowed richness to our repertory of wilderness encounters that lingers in our souls.

The Merit of Lesser Known Trails and the Virtue of Short Hikes

While hiking often focuses on the well-known wild and primitive backcountry, unexpectedly-rewarding hiking experiences can be attained in relatively tame areas which are often obscure or overlooked, such as the Cumberland Gap National Historical Park. The Cumberland Gap!! The name drips with history as a wilderness tamed by intrepid pioneers. For the Indians, it was the Warrior's Path and was discovered by Dr. Thomas Walker in 1750. Of course its fame comes from Daniel Boone leading settlers through the Gap to the "Dark and Bloody Ground" of Kentucky. Unfortunately from the viewpoint of hikers, it was also a proving ground in the 1930s that a paved road could be built in this kind of terrain. Happily, this situation was remedied in 1996, when the highway was relocated to a tunnel through the mountain and the original road closed and dismantled. Thus the Gap is being restored to resemble its pioneer days as the Wilderness Road. The park itself was established in 1955 and has about 20,000 acres.

The Gap is at the west end of the park, and the park itself is a long plateau that rises 1000 feet above the valley floor. A trail runs along the top of the ridge for some twenty miles, but the more fascinating hiking destinations are in the eastern part of the park. Throughout the southern mountains are many preserved or restored areas to show what mountain life was like before modern advantages took it all away. It was a hard life that few would want to live today—but the endurance and integrity of the mountaineers is a wonder to behold. One such example has been restored in the park in the form of the Hensley Settlement that can only be reached by hiking or by a poor road that requires a four-wheel drive. It is said that this is the "last pioneer settlement in the Eastern United

States" because it was not started until 1904 but eventually had twelve farms and nearly one-hundred people at its peak in the 1930's. This was a very isolated community with no real roads leading to it, perhaps so that moonshine could be made without unnecessary interference. It was a hard haul up and down the mountain on foot or horseback to bring in items needed by an otherwise very self-sufficient people. But the appeal of modern life away from this remaining bastion of isolated life proved greater and the settlement was abandoned in the 1950s. In recent years, the Park Service has restored three of the homesteads to reestablish the farms to nearly original conditions, including fields planted with crops typical of the times and a renovated school house and cemetery. The Park Service has farmer-demonstrators living at the site to do the work and explain this fading lifestyle.

Tourists can see mountain homesteads in the Smokies, but the traffic and the crowds make it difficult to picture what it might have been like. At Hensley Settlement one can stroll around the farms with only the sounds of the birds or of the farm work being done. As one looks in the cabin and wanders the fields, a sense of the slow pace of life can be envisaged before the rush of modern times ended isolation for all of us. The picture is not totally realistic in that the noise of children, the bay of dogs, and the commotion and smell of farm animals is not present, and a reading of the headstones in the cemetery reminds one how grim that life could be. However, one comes away with a renewed sense of well-being to even briefly touch on the life our forefathers built and maintained with backbreaking work.

The Park Service does offer a van trip to the site, but the way to experience it is the way the people at that time did and walk the Chadwell Gap Trail for the four miles to the settlement. On one trip my wife and I were breathing heavily as we hiked toward the top of the plateau where the settlement exists when we were astonished to see a small girl walking towards us without any adults around. We discovered that she was four years old. When we asked her what she was doing, she replied that her mother and father worked on the farm at the settlement and she was on her way to visit her grandma, who lived at the start of the trail. She said she did this walk often by herself. As she continued on her way we could only marvel that the independent spirit of the folks at Hensley was still very much alive.

On another occasion I took a church group of twelve-year-old boys and several adults on an overnight hike to this area. The Park Service has a primitive cabin at Martins Fork that can be reserved for a modest fee. This was my first time in leading a group; therefore, I tried to instruct them on proper equipment prior to our hike. Alas, when the day came and we were all assembled at the trail head, I realized it was a mistake not to pay greater attention to the details. They had an appalling collection of gear, with one adult carrying Kool-Aid in glass jars. There was no choice but to press on, secure in the knowledge that the cabin was only three miles away, albeit uphill; we could still dump all this gear in the cabin and explore with a minimum of equipment. My weary party was able to make it to the cabin. We had a delightful day roaming the fields of Hensley Settlement and a restless night at the cabin as the boys discovered that mice were the rightful owners of the place.

Some four miles from the cabin, towards the end of the park, is one of the finest but almost unknown geological features of the Appalachians— Sand Cave. It is not a true cave but a huge bluff with an arch 300 feet long and 100 feet high in front, with an area of over an acre of sand inside the "cave." The arch in front is an impressive array of rocks and columns of varying colors, rather like some ancient ruin. Inside, the walls and sand are of different colors to make a display more reminiscent of the Far West. As the sand floor inside the cave is sloped, the boys had a good time running and rolling down the sand. Also nearby are the cliffs of White Rocks which look impressive and foreboding from the valley floor below and were a major landmark to the early pioneers. One never knows the impact one can have with such an outing, but years later one of the boys, now a college student, came to my house to get a map of the area to visit it again for a hiking trip with friends.

The vast majority of trails I have hiked are ones that are old, often a half-century or more, so it is rare to be able to hike on a new trail. My wife and I hiked the new Wilderness Road trail in Cumberland Gap only a month after it opened. The Park Service has the goal to return the area to the state as experienced by the original pioneers but the land where a major paved road existed takes some time to reclaim its natural condition. The "new" Wilderness Road twists back and forth over where the road existed. The road bed has been reconfigured to its natural contours, but still has a very man-made appearance about it. The restored hillside has a gentle smooth look that has been seeded in grass. Some time will elapse before it returns to the state of wildness as witnessed by Daniel Boone and company. But nature can do wonders in a few decades. In the Smokies one can drive the gravel Parsons Branch Road from Cades Cove where, prior to the establishment of the park, there was extensive farming; yet as you drive through this jungle, it is difficult to envisage it with cleared fields and vibrant homesteads. If man disappeared from the earth, aliens who arrived a few hundred years later would have to do some serious digging to find evidence of our existence; such are the powers of nature we keep temporally at bay.

At the southwestern toe of Virginia, the state's many magnificent mountains reach their climax, both in height at 5729-foot high Mt. Rogers and in a distinctive state park called Grayson Highlands. Because it is a state park, it does not receive the recognition of a national park like the Smokies, or commercial sites such as Grandfather Mountain and the famous Rock City with all the familiar road signs. A Westerner used to the wide-open landscape of the Rockies and the desert might not be impressed with Grayson Highlands, but to an Easterner it is a precious gem. Years ago the area was heavily logged, then burned and kept clear for pastures, resulting in a barren upland with huge granite boulders in profusion and only a few trees to block the sweeping views of the highest mountains of Virginia.

Grayson Highlands Park was established in 1965 and the decision was made to keep it in meadows and rocky outcroppings rather than restore it to its original forest-covered state. Initially the vegetation was kept in check by a sheep herd, but now, picturesquely it is grazed by a herd of wild horses that live there all year. There are trails in the park, but in this open land, one can ramble where the mood strikes without fear of being lost and enjoying a continually changing view. The jumbled rocks and rugged exposed terrain reminds all that beneath the gently rolling mountains of the Appalachians lie a tormented and commanding mass of granite that is only thinly covered by flora that have fought for centuries to wrestle a life-hold in a hostile land.

Robert and I made an overnight trip hiking this section of the AT with uninterrupted views in all directions of the surrounding tree-covered mountains and ended our hike at Mt. Rogers, the highest point in Virginia. Unfortunately there was no view from atop that peak and we hiked back to the treeless area to camp in a spacious open meadow. We could find no campsite with a source of water, so we were forced to be very conservative in our use of this precious liquid. We had enough to use for drinking and cooking, but we could not wash ourselves or our eating utensils as I would like. Sometimes cleanliness can be overrated. We settled down for the night, and while trying to go to sleep I started thinking about the wild horses. As we were camped in an open pasture, my mind started to wonder if horses sleep at night in one place or engage in social events like stampedes and if they can see an orange tent at night. Fortunately we were not trampled under an avalanche of hooves that night and resolved to return to this serene area again.

Not far from Nashville, Tennessee, is a singular hiking area that has an enchanted forest charm about it that rivals any fairy tale. It is the

Virgin Falls Pocket Wilderness created by the Bowater paper company. Commercial foresters often have a bad reputation among hikers, but Bowater had taken several outstanding natural sites in their extensive forest holdings and set aside these areas with the pledge of no lumbering in them. They developed them for hikers by constructing hiking trails and campsites. The 317-acre area of Virgin Falls would almost qualify as a miniature national park, such are its distinctive features. In 1996, it was acquired by the State of Tennessee and preserved under the Natural Areas Program.

On one of our trips to Virgin Falls, Robert and I drove to the parking area that is two miles up a dirt road and undeterred by the fact that rain was forecast for the weekend. The trail to Virgin Falls is the reverse of the average hiking trail in that it starts at the top of a plateau and goes down. This escarpment is where the western end of the plateau drops into the flat areas of middle Tennessee and has rugged terrain for many miles at the edge. Also, unlike so many hiking trails that may have only one interesting feature, this trail rewards the hiker with a constant variety. As one descends into the heavily forested gorge, one encounters Big Branch Falls, Caney Fork Overlook, Big Laurel Falls, and Sheep Cave before coming to the highpoint of the hike.

Virgin Falls is an exquisite jewel in that it sits alone without an apparent stream. The water flows out of a cave a short distance, drops into a small cone-shaped basin and disappears into the sinkhole at the base of the falls. The scene is as enthralling as any I have ever encountered. The falls seemingly exist by magic without any connection to a tributary. The falls are surrounded by lush vegetation in its own small valley, and to hike down to the base where the water disappears twirling around the rocks is to stand in a misty realm that seems apart from the entire world. It is a mystical moment to look up at the cascading falls while engulfed in the spray that has created the flora of a Garden of Eden on three sides and to briefly exist beyond time and place.

We set up our tents at a campsite on the Caney Fork River and listened to the rain all night and hiked out the next morning. When we arrived back at the car we found the nocturnal rains had turned the dirt road into a continuous ribbon of mud. I was driving my big Buick Century, which was a powerful car, but it handled badly in slippery conditions. After surveying the situation, we concluded the only way out was to hit the muddy road at a high speed and accelerate as fast as we could or we would be stuck like an ox in a ditch miles from any help. I took advantage of the dry ground of the parking lot to floor the gas pedal and we assaulted the mud full blast. As we rocked along, twisting from one side of the muddy road to the other, I felt more like I was steering a boat in choppy waters than driving a car. The mud soon covered the windshield so that the wipers were unable to combat such a constant barrage and I was forced to look out one side window and Robert out the other, yelling when I got too close to exiting on his side into the forest and beyond. My great fear was that a car or truck might be coming the other way. In such an unhappy encounter, a collision would be inevitable. Fortunately we made it down the two miles of miry slush without mishap.

Normally I prefer to hike in new places rather than return to where I have been because part of the joy of hiking is the discovery of unexpected landscapes. Virgin Falls, however, is a place one can return to again and again. It is never the same on each trip, for depending on the amount of rainfall in the days prior to the hike; the falls can roar with all the authority of tons of water brooking no interference or be a gentle trickle down a rock wall. On another trip, Robert and I returned with our young daughters and had an idyllic time that creates the memories that never cease. At the river campsite, there was a rope hanging invitingly from a tree, strategically placed over the a deep pool meant for swimming, and the girls spent joyful time swinging out from the bank, letting go and plunging into the cool waters.

The well-publicized trails have their rewards, but a venture into the obscure means greater solitude and a taste of superb panoramas known to a relative few. The realm of footpaths far and near in the United States offers an astonishing variety that no hiker, no matter how committed, can exhaust. For many years, I was of the opinion that a true hike had to be at least four miles or more; anything shorter was a mere stroll and less than a true nature experience. This opinion was tempered by the fact that a hike to the top of the Chimneys in the Smokies is only a mile and a half, but because of the steepness of this trail it is one of the more challenging in the park. However, even a short walk in the forest can bring a change of mood and a new perspective on life. Just venturing off a road and a few feet into the woods seems to transform my very being. For even a brief moment, I cease to be part of the man-made world and go into the realm of Gaia more real than the province of concrete and steel. Looking around and seeing only trees, rocks, and streams makes me focus on a higher reality bereft of all human created concerns. The two extremes of man's existence connect. One is the primitive side before civilization that must cope with survival against powerful forces that are part of the truly real world, even if this feeling may be illusory if one is only fifty feet from a highway. The other is the higher world beyond our narrow self-interest and petty quarrels, and to face our smallest in the cosmos as our dwellings is but a small scratch on our planet's surface that would be shortly gone if we were not here to maintain our temporary creations, all this from just stepping away briefly from normal urban-suburban life into Nature's domain.

The highest peak in the Great Smoky Mountain National Park is Clingmans Dome at an elevation of 6642 feet, and it is also the tallest point on the entire Appalachian Trail. However, there is rarely solitude on this summit unless you are there in the winter when the road to the nearby parking lot is closed. A paved trail of a half mile leads from the parking area to the modernistic foot tower at the top, so this mass of humanity is not representative of typical hikers. Nevertheless, over the years it has been a pleasant trip to take visitors from the flatlands to give them a sample of the splendor of the park and take some pride in walking to top of the Smokies. As it is four-hundred feet, all uphill, it can be a challenge for those unaccustomed to any short ascent, but the panorama from the top can be inspiring. This hike was one of my earliest and one of my most frequent over the years. Alarmingly, the area has changed dramatically from the sixties when I made my first trip to this summit. Where once it was a full mature forest, it is now littered with the sterile tree skeletons of dead Spruce Firs, killed from the invasion of an accidentally-imported insect called the balsam woolly adelgid from central Europe. Even a man-protected forest can change over time from man's unplanned activities.

There are some walks that hardly qualify as a hike, yet create memories of a lifetime. Early in our marriage, I had the dilemma of how to entertain Amos, my newly acquired father-in-law. He was not the hiker type, so I would drive him around East Tennessee to fathom his interests. On one of these sojourns, I drove him through Chickamauga Battlefield in North Georgia. He was fascinated and allowed how his grandfather, Sam Ward, had fought in the Civil War and wondered if he had been in this battle. Upon later research, we learned that he was with the 58th Ohio Regiment, had not been at Chickamauga, but had fought and was wounded at the battle of Shiloh in West Tennessee. On a later in-law visit, Amos and I went to Shiloh National Military Park and the staff of the park headquarters was most helpful in showing where the 58th Ohio had been in the battle. They were part of the Third Division commanded by General Lew Wallace (later to write *Ben Hur*), who was ordered to march to Shiloh but got lost on backroads and arrived too late for the first day of the battle but were part of the action on the second day. Amos and I were able to start our walk where his grandfather camped that night and then follow the progress of the regiment as they forced back the Southern lines, until in the middle of the woods. we came upon a stone memorial to the 58th Ohio. As we traversed the ground his grandfather had fought for over a hundred years ago, we tried to imagine the ordeal of this young eighteen-year-old. Old battlefields are deceptively quiet, as they are well-maintained parks with many monuments and markers in a serene setting of forest and fields. Yet the reality of that terrible day of blood, fear and courage is difficult to comprehend in such a tranquil surrounding. Alas, Sam Ward survived the Civil War only to be killed by a bull on his farm in Missouri. In telling about this brief stroll, my father-in-law would later say of all the things he had done in his life, that visit to Shiloh was his favorite. In subsequent years, I repeated the trip to Shiloh with my wife, never a military history fan, but she also was greatly moved to walk over this same hallowed ground that her great-grandfather had so agonizingly advanced across in face of shot and shell.

Even in the densely-populated area of Atlanta there is a unique geological feature that invites the wanderer to ramble— the imposing granite monolith of Stone Mountain, rising some 825 feet above the flat Georgia countryside. There is no solitude found here, as the park includes an 1870s recreated village; a scenic railroad around the mountain; a Confederate memorial carved into its side featuring Jefferson Davis, Robert E. Lee and "Stonewall" Jackson and a cable car to the visitor center at the top of the mountain that will guarantee no seclusion once the summit is reached. But it is fascinating to thread one's way up the 1.3-mile trail of largely bare rock with gradually unfolding views of the surrounding landscape and urbanscape. This mountain of rock is some 300 million years old and provides ample opportunity to reflect on our finite existence while studying the effects of countless years of erosion on the seemingly impervious granite surface and the valiant attempt of vegetation to secure a foothold. The reward of the view from the top is to see the outline of Atlanta in the distance and the satisfaction of seeing the considerable pastoral surroundings that still remain despite the urban expansion so prominent in this area. This short hike of a continuous ascent will exercise the lungs and leg muscles while providing an intriguing surrounding not often experienced in the Eastern United States.

As with the uncontested meander across the Shiloh Battlefield, some hikes are more noteworthy for their historical significance than for an encounter with nature in the raw. One such hike involved a mundane forest setting. I had volunteered to be an Ambassador for the American Hiking Society, the only nationwide group solely dedicated to the creation and preservation of hiking trails. As my first activity on behalf of that organization, I was allowed to speak at the dedication of the newly restored two-and-a-half mile section of the Unicoi Turnpike Trail near Coker Creek, Tennessee. This route across the mountains between Tennessee and North Carolina was used for centuries by the Indians and later developed into the main link of the Atlantic coastal plains to the Cherokee territories, with a commercial wagon road being constructed in the early 1800s. According to the handout about the trail, "Segments of this historic road remain intact on forest service lands-representing what is likely the oldest intact roadbed on public lands in the nation." The thrill of walking on such a historic path is tempered in part by some of its dark past, as this was the first leg of the Trail of Tears, the removal of the Cherokees on a forced trek from this area to Oklahoma. At the dedication, a woman of Cherokee descent recounted the history of Cherokee cooperation with the newcomers, including saving the life of Andrew Jackson at a battle. The Cherokees constructed settlements and farms similar to the pioneers, and Sequoyah invented a Cherokee alphabet, a monumental intellectually achievement and soon the Cherokees had published their own newspaper. Despite all this, the pressure for their land and the gold in the area resulted in President Jackson ordering their removal, a diaspora that started across this trail. This sad episode of man's cruelty to man lingers over the forest as if ghosts from the past still protest this injustice, a walk on a short trail with a lengthy legacy.

The first time I went to Joyce Kilmer Memorial Forest was with my wife in the early years of our marriage. This area was set aside because it had never been logged and is a rare example of the virgin forest in Eastern United States. In addition to longer trails, there is a short two-mile stroll that allows you to sample the magnificence of primeval America. The tulip poplar trees, many over nine feet around with a canopy one-hundred-fifty feet above the ground, create the impression that one is in a natural cathedral. Midway through the hike is a plaque to Joyce Kilmer, to whom the forest is dedicated, with his poem "Trees":

> I think that I shall never see
> A poem lovely as a tree.
> A tree whose hungry mouth is prest
> Against the sweet earth's flowing breast;
> A tree that may in summer wear
> A nest of robins in her hair;
>
> A tree that looks at God all day,
> And lifts her leafy arms to pray;
> Upon whose bosom snow has lain;
> Who intimately lives with rain,
> Poems are made by fools like me,
> But only God can make a tree.

Walking in such a setting brings the poem alive. One can begin to imagine the magnificent wilderness the Eastern United States must have been before man's intervention.

Some trails come to mean more than a walk in the woods and become part of your very fabric and are repeated time and again in different settings of our life. The Laurel Falls Trail is a mere five-mile drive from

Gatlinburg, where we frequently go for dinner and entertainment. One can stroll on this trail in almost any attire and its briefness allows the time to fit in with any other activities. The Laurel Falls Trail meanders through an attractive lowland forest for only a mile and ascends gradually to arrive at an exuberant cascade of fifty feet that is most satisfying to view up close, particularly after a rainy period. On the trail, the laurel and rhododendron can be profuse in June and give a garden-like setting, and even bears can be seen by chance. We like to hike it in the different seasons to experience the diverse moods that come with the timeless cycles of nature.

The down-side of this pleasant stroll is that because it is short and goes to an attractive destination the trail became worn out and the Park Service paved it over so that it would be usable. With a paved trail, the likelihood of becoming lost is remote even for the true novice, and even the physically unskilled can manage this section for a taste of the park away from the windshield tour of the park. Even that can be for a daunting task for those not adjusted to walking up hill. We saw a family with the husband, who was in his forties and not overweight, nevertheless pausing for breath only a fourth of the way to Laurel Falls. Not sure if they ever made it. But if one is prepared for the crowds, this short path is as good as anyone will encounter in the Smokies, dedicated to the creed that any walk in the woods, however short, is a positive experience in life.

The Joy of Hiking

Many times when I describe my hiking experiences I receive a quizzical look that asks why I willingly indulge in such a pastime, as if I am a disciple of Marquis de Sade. For those who will drive endlessly around the shopping center parking lot in a desperate search for the space three places closer to the entrance, it is a puzzling aberration to hear such tales of a willingness to walk. On the other hand, there are those of more intense sports— the mountain climber, the Ironman triathlon participant, and the cross country runner, who affect a look of bemusement for my stories, as if listening to a young boy excitedly describing the first train he has seen. Somewhere in the middle of this spectrum is where I have found my deep satisfaction.

The rewards of hiking and its occasional pain exist on many different levels. The lure of hiking that keeps me returning to the woods is the kinescope of its facets, a diamond that when rotated in the light has many variations. It can be both comical and life-threatening; mundane and inspiring; body strengthening and exhausting. It represents much of life, with long periods of routine trudging on the trail and mind-numbing tedium punctuated with high points such as an unexpected beautiful vista, a brief sight of an animal in the wild, a helpful act or word from another person, and in some extreme cases a reminder of our own mortality.

One dimension of the forest is the encounters with nature that are largely foreign to modern man in his cocoon of protection against any extremes, a security that is only occasionally penetrated and then featured prominently on the evening news as a disaster. Man in the modern world has sought to overpower and neutralize nature in order to remove its total control over him. To be sure, hiking on a trail created by man, with helpful signs at its junctions and awareness that there are rangers available to assist in dire straits, is to not completely leave the human realm and to see the world as primitive man might; it is a taste of the timelessness of it all that is entrancing. One still voluntarily surrenders control of significant elements of life to be measured by the forces as they exist apart from our sheltered existence. It is a reality known to our ancestors and, unfortunately, by too many of the world's poor.

To be a part of nature one quickly learns the importance of weather. Setting off on a day hike, one has a reasonably good assurance of what to expect. If it is clear in the entire region, one can assume that the sky will be bright. However, mountains are notoriously tricky in their weather and conditions can quickly develop of awesome proportions. In the lowlands, the weather may be pleasant all day, while an appalling storm envelops the mountaintop. Fallen trees across the trail are mute reminders of the consequences when the savage winds blow through the mountains. In the winter, the ordeals of even the most experienced hikers who have perished in the snow and the cold are in one's mind. Yet the weather is part of the experience and to be part of it, in subtle ways, is a reward in itself. With only your clothes and the thin fabric of a tent by night, you are truly a part of the elements.

The knowledge of the nature of the terrain is also of great importance in the preparation for the journey. Is the trail well-marked and what are the sources of water? What is the elevation gain and is it continuous or is one constantly gaining and losing the heights? There is joy in life of the unplanned and spontaneous, but in the wilds, especially in the winter, or on a trip of several days, the joy of the impromptu is but a mask that shields misery or a darker fate. One cannot plan for all possibilities, but a firm knowledge and sensible preparation for likely possibilities is a key to confidence if adversity comes— a lesson well applied in all of life.

The animals in the woods give one the impression of trying to pursue their primeval life cycles despite the infringement of man. They have little choice but to live in our world, even in a national park and they respond by avoiding us, ignoring us, or beholding us as an opportunity to secure food. Those animals hunted in the national forests will not be seen in hunting season, but those in the national parks view us with indifference or annoyance. Here there are no affable dogs or cats eager to be our friends, but animals that live free where we are the intruders. But there is delight to meet them in their homes and to accommodate to them rather than acting as if they are in our world.

Another aspect of hiking is entering into a different relationship with strangers. One can read that in ancient time and frontier days a traveler could knock on a strange door and be welcomed in for the night. Societies still exist that place a high premium on hospitability to strangers, but it has largely vanished in a cloud of suspicion in the Western world. On the trail these old traditions are resurrected, be it in sharing of food or supplies, information on the next water source, what to expect further on the trail or simply the joy of a shared experience apart from the modern world.

It is said that men in combat develop a kinship that can run deeper than blood relationship. The reason is simple in that your life depends on the actions of your fellow soldiers and their lives on you. I have never served in the military, but in hiking you develop a deeper bond with your companion because there is a certain interdependence. It may be as simple as his bringing supplies that you forgot or as critical as a potentially life-threatening situation.

There is a deeper appreciation of those in authority and service. Someone had to plan out these trails and young hard muscles went into their construction Many trails in the Smokies were built by those unemployed during the Depression and grateful for the work. Those who control wilderness do this task to maintain it for optimum enjoyment. One may grumble at the necessity of getting a permit, but without it the quality could deteriorate rapidly.

Hiking affects one's outlook on life in many ways. As a modern man with many of the conveniences that are considered necessities, it was in amazement that I discovered I could carry on my back all the requirements to live reasonably comfortably for a week. To live this way all the time is not desired, but it is the break from civilization that refreshes, so one can return to the race with our competitive species and face it all with renewed spirit.

There are, of course, issues of how much modern life should intrude upon life on the trail. When I started hiking, someone bringing a radio was the only real concern, an occurrence that was exceedingly rare and would make one a pariah. With advanced technology, the possibility of being isolated from the rest of humanity is becoming very remote. Some are good, but are still viewed with mixed emotions. In the past, one had a map and a compass to help if directions became confusing. Now with a GPS and good maps, theoretically, one would never be lost, and with cell phones, assuming there is a tower somewhere in range, help can be summoned in very short time. Still some unspoken quality is lost with the lessening of risks and solitude. One long distance solo hiker I read about combated loneliness by bringing her iPod with a solar-powered recharger to help counter long and uneventful hours on the trail. The wilderness has certainly become less wild and one will never be removed from contacts with other mortals; such is the price of our ever-advancing civilization.

If one is to pursue hiking as a lifelong pastime, there is the requirement to keep reasonably in shape. This is not a hobby where one can gain excessive weight or be a couch potato in the intervals between hikes, if one has any expectation of enjoying or even being capable of the next hike. Thus, the sport demands a relatively healthy lifestyle if it is to be savored, as one discovers with passing years how brief life truly is. As I do not hike often enough for that to be my main source of conditioning, other means are necessary. The logical and healthy solution is regular walks wherever I live or visit. Happily, I live in a large subdivision that is hilly, so there are many roads with limited traffic and inclines sufficient to condition me on a routine basis.

There is one major drawback to walking the byways of a neighborhood, namely the supposedly domesticated canine population. The premier hiker in the Bible, Paul the Apostle, who must have walked a thousand miles in his missionary journeys and who should know, warned in Philippians 3:2, "Beware of dogs..." Now some theologians place other interpretations on that passage, but I prefer to take it literally. I am very fond of friendly dogs, but many see it as their duty to protect their owner's property, which sometimes they unfortunately interpret as the road in front of the house. I do not have a great fear of dogs, which has probably been a factor in having never been bitten. This calmness was important when sauntering near our first home; I was suddenly surrounded by ten or more dogs in a pack. Feeling somewhat like a wounded caribou with a team of wolves circling for the kill, I couldn't think of anything to do but stand completely still. To run would incite them and to kick at one would likely unleash more excitement from the rest, who undoubtedly never had anger management classes. Happily none bit me and I started to slowly walk away with constant barking all around me. Shortly they tired of the game and ran off, but I resolved to do what I could to protect myself in future walks.

That great outdoorsman, Teddy Roosevelt, said, "Walk softly and carry a big stick," or words to that effect. The power of a heavy wooden staff on a dog's psyche is amazing. Many would approach but stay at a safe distance. After the county passed a leash law that all dogs must be restrained, the incidents of dog encounters dropped and I sometimes walked without a staff. On one street, however, there was an unleashed little dog that liked to run off his porch and make a great demonstration of his ferocity. However, when I did carry a threatening truncheon he would sit calmly on his porch as if totally unaware of my passing in front of his house. The best solution however is a modern invention, the handy dandy, super duper, doggy zapper. This commercial handheld device emits a high-pitched sound that humans can't detect but is agonizing to the sensitive hearing of dogs. The effect is truly amazing; a dog may be running at me all bark and fury, when I let him have a zap the dog bounds back as if he had hit an invisible wall and looks around in demoralized confusion. It has the great advantage of not hurting the dog and the even greater advantage of leaving large and potentially hostile dog owners puzzled about the situation. I still carry my stick, however, in the event I should encounter a deaf dog.

Even hiking in the confines of my own neighborhood can produce bizarre results, a locality that I have lived here much longer than most of the residents. After leaving TVA and recovering from a period of ill health, I decided one winter day to return to walking the surrounding blocks. In preparation, I decided there was no need to shave or wear good clothes that would get sweaty. As I would only be a short distance from home, I saw no point in carrying my wallet. My loving wife advised me against this approach, but I put on old clothes and a new black cap given to me by TVA police as a retirement gift and cheerfully headed out. As I trekked along, I waved at my neighbors driving past on their way to work, a duty that was temporarily not mine. The fact that they failed to wave back was not a deterrent to my pleasant mood. About half-way through my walk a police cruiser pulled up in front of me, and out stepped the officer of the law. Rather gruffly, he said, "We have a report of a prowler in the area wearing a black cap." "Gee officer I haven't seen anyone else walking in the vicinity," I innocently responded. Then the terrible truth occurred that he was talking about me! About that time a second cruiser pulled up. I guess the report was of one mean hombre, and a back-up was necessary. Indignantly, I replied that I had lived in the neighborhood for years. Softening, the officer said, "Fine, just show me some identification." Spirits sinking, I was forced to confess that I'd left my wallet at home. During further discourse, he kept looking at my cap with the TVA police emblems on it and finally I said, "Look, I will get in the police car if you like and you can drive me to my home and I will go in and get my driver's license." He shrugged and said, "No need, you don't look like a prowler," and got back in his car and left me in peace. After that I was always a well-dressed stroller with plenty of identification but with a smoldering resentment of the neighborhood quisling who ratted on me.

Sadly, even a lifetime of reasonably consciousness exercise cannot overcome the dictates of genetics. My father died of a heart attack in his fifties and I have always run a high cholesterol level, so I knew a day of reckoning would come. In order to keep in shape between hikes, one routine is lifting-weights. There is a debate between aerobic exercise such as walking and strength training such as weight lifting as to the best one for the human body, but as so often in life it is not a choice between the two— both are necessary and beneficial. It was during one such exercise with barbells that I once again experienced the pain of my chosen hobby when I dropped a 25-pound barbell on my big toe. The pain was severe and an unpleasant sensation persisted so that I went to my doctor and discovered the weight had broken a toe. The cure was to wear a wooden shoe that allowed no movement and certainly limited my walking. Little did I know that this accident may well have saved my life. Prior to that unfortunate incident I had started to feel a shortness of breath on even short walks but attributed it to being out of shape. On one trip returning home from Nashville, but still wearing this cumbersome chuck of wood on my foot, I decided to pull off the interstate and walk to Burgess Falls, which required only a short walk from the parking lot to the overlook. While enjoying the spectacle of this most beautiful falls I was tempted to hike down to its base some one-hundred feet below but decided that with my injured foot the climb back up to the trail would be too great a strain in my condition.

Even with my limitations of a broken toe, I continued to experience a shortness of breath. When I didn't need to wear the wooden shoe anymore, I felt so bad as to not even be able to make the short roundtrip to Laurel Falls. My wife prevailed upon me to see my doctor who ordered stress tests. When I went in the next day for the results he said, "You are going to the hospital right now; you have significant blockage in your heart." In the ensuing operation, two stents were placed in my artery that had a ninety-five percent blockage. Later I learned that that artery is referred to as the "widow maker." I still live because trying to do activities related to my hobby alerted me and others to a pending life-threatening condition. The pain of hiking allowed me to continue to know the joy of life.

Of course, there are risks in hiking and one develops a heightened awareness of one's surroundings. I often walk around lost in my thoughts and oblivious to what is happening around me, but I can't do that when hiking. The first requirement is careful attention to where you are going for to wander off the trail in an Eastern forest, particularly in the Smokies, is to invite disaster, especially when only equipped for a day hike. The way is not always clear and the path may be faint or branch off in different directions, so watchful focus is constantly called for. As there may be animals about, you must develop an instinct for movement around you. This vigilant attention to the environment is a useful trait whether on the trail, in the subways of Paris, or in ordinary life.

The wonder of discovery in walking about leads to observations often missed. The slow pace of walking allows one to take in much more than would otherwise be discovered. Even near my home I am amazed at what I notice in walks that I have missed driving by a hundred times. There is even a management philosophy of work that emphasizes leaving the office, walking around unplanned and spontaneously talking to people at all levels for their perspectives or their attitudes and how things can be done differently. Managers that take this approach are often some of the most effective and so it is in life that casually walking about alerts one to many things that otherwise would be missed.

I am a different person because I like to walk. Walking became a habit in my youth because it was my main form of exercise. On long solitary walks, one becomes a reflective person and there is much time to reflect on the "big questions of life" and time to brood on the petty insults. It was my fate in my early life not to be immersed in constant activities of family, sports, and TV viewing. If I had become so inner-focused without my limitations and long walks I do not know, but I feel that I have touched parts of my intuitive being that would forever be reclusive without the private strolls on foot through city streets and forest glens.

Hiking is a wonderful hobby but the wonder is the break with civilization. One's thoughts focus on the basics such as *where is the next source of water* and *am I heading correctly* and *will I be where I need to be before it is dark.* Nature controls as it rarely does in civilization unless it is at its extreme, such as a hurricane or earthquake. Even in the best of days one does not lose the awareness that you are in Nature's temple and will live by what it dictates. In some ways it puts you in touch with our ancestors. Our civilization is only a few thousand years old and even today there are many who live this way. The recently-passed mountaineers, whose log cabins one sees in shambles or in a specially-preserved state to be viewed by the tourist, become not uncultured "hillbillies" to make fun of, but hardy and ingenious souls that used what was at hand to build a life that could sample at least some of the joys and comforts we take for granted.

I would not choose hiking for everyday existence, but it is the break that is meaningful with the knowledge that one can return to it. Hardships are only interesting if they are voluntarily endured and can be ended at choice. To live in primitive conditions constantly would only narrow one's horizon, while to experience primitive conditions occasionally broadens them.

As the years roll on, there is yet time to hike the Milford in New Zealand or the arctic paths on Baffin Island before the infirmities of the body put a quietus to such endeavors and leave only the memories and the mental images of such times in the wilderness. But I am confident that even in the beyond there will be new walks to take and new wonders to explore down some shaded path.

About the Author

David Curran lives in Powell, TN with his wife, Lola. He was born in Pennsylvania and lived there until his family moved to Florida when he was eleven. He graduated with a BA from Florida State University and a MA from the University of Kentucky. He worked for the Tennessee Valley Authority, mainly in Human Resources, for 28 years in the Knoxville, Tennessee area. Later he was an instructor in management courses at Carson-Newman College and Tennessee Wesleyan College for four years. David and his wife served as missionaries for the International Mission Board-Southern Baptist Convention in Paris, France for a year and a half. They have two daughters, Gina and Elizabeth, and two grandsons, William and Andrew, who are happily taking an interest in hiking and backpacking.

You can find more information about David Curran and photographs of his hiking adventures at: www.hikingforfunandpain.com

CPSIA information can be obtained
at www.ICGtesting.com
Printed in the USA
LVHW010200230819
628523LV00001B/4